SCOTS IN POLAND, RUSSIA AND THE BALTIC STATES
[Part Four]

By
David Dobson

Copyright © 2021
by David Dobson
All Rights Reserved

Published for Clearfield Company by
Genealogical Publishing Company
Baltimore, Maryland
2021

ISBN 9780806359250

INTRODUCTION

The links between Scotland and the countries lying along the southern shores of the Baltic can be traced back as far as the Medieval period when Scottish knights accompanied the Teutonic knights on their Baltic Crusade against the heathen Letts. Since then various economic links encouraged merchants to settle in the main seaports, such as Danzig alias Gdansk. The main period of Scottish settlement, however, occurred from around 1560 to about 1650.

The catalyst for much of this emigration of Scots to Poland was the economic opportunity created by the socio-economic gap between the Polish aristocracy and the peasantry. This gap was filled mainly by German, Dutch, Scots and Jewish entrepreneurs. Religious liberty in Poland, for much of the period, attracted immigrants who, in their own right, had been subject to persecution in their homelands. Many of the Scots who settled initially along the shores of the Baltic had arrived as soldiers of fortune recruited to fight for and against the armies of Poland, Russia, and Sweden. Choosing to remain in Poland, these veterans later settled on lands given for service rendered, or as itinerant *cramers* or pedlars. During the seventeenth century there was hardly a locality in Poland that did not contain some Scots. By the 1640s it was reckoned that there were approximately 30,000 Scots resident in Poland – one of the greatest concentrations of Scots in continental Europe. By the middle of the seventeenth century the appeal of Poland and the Baltic lands began to wane for Scottish emigrants, who were discouraged by the Cossack and other wars, and encouraged by opportunities to the west – initially in Ireland and later in America.

Although economic links between Scotland and the Baltic lands have grown since the sixteenth century, far fewer Scots chose to settle there. Some Scots returned home in due course, but many chose to remain in Poland-Lithuania. Scottish surnames--often modified--can be found in local records, such as the baptismal and marriage records of the churches in Konigsberg, now Kaliningrad. In more recent times substantial numbers of Poles and other people from the Baltic have settled in Scotland.

This volume marks the fourth in a series. It is based on numerous primary and second sources found in the British Isles and continental Europe, including the Aberdeen City Archives, the Dundee Shipping Lists, the Danish Archives (Copenhagen), and *The Scottish Community in the Grand Duchy of Lithuania, 1630-1750*, by Michael Broun Ayre.

David Dobson, Dundee, 2021.

REFERENCES

ACA   Aberdeen City Archives

AJ   Aberdeen Journal, series

ASW   Aberdeen Shore Works Accounts, 1596-1670, L. B.Taylor, Aberdeen, 1972

BL   British Library, London

CTB   Calendar of Treasury Books

DCA   Dundee City Archives

DSL   Dundee Shipping Lists

HS   History Scotland, series

JSM   Geschichte der Koniglich Preussischen See and Handelsstadt Memel.

MD   Mariners of Dundee, H. Robertson, Dundee, 2006

NRS   National Records of Scotland, Edinburgh

PL   Port of Leith, Sue Mowat, Edinburgh, 197-

PRONI   Public Record Office of Northern Ireland, Belfast

RAK   Danish Archives, Copenhagen

RGS   Register of the Great Seal of Scotland

S   Scotsman, series

SAP   Scotland and Poland, Devine & Hesse, Edinburgh, 2011

SCA   Scottish Communities Abroad....., Grosjean & Murdoch, Leiden, 2005

SCL   The Scottish Community in the Grand Duchy of Lithuania, 1630-1750. Michael Broun Ayre, Vilnius, 2019**

SCM   Miscellany of the Spalding Club, Aberdeen, 1841

SHR Scottish Historical Review, series
SIS Scots in Sweden, Berg & Lagercrantz, Stockholm, 1962
SRS Scottish Records Society

SCOTS IN POLAND, RUSSIA &

THE BALTIC STATES IV

ABBOT, KEITH EDWARD, consul general in Odessa, 1835-1843. [NRS.GD371.122]

ABERCROMBIE, ANDREW, master of the Fox of Dundee trading between Konigsberg and Dundee in 1616. [DSL]

ABERCROMBIE, JAMES, master of the Isabel of Dundee, trading between Riga and Dundee in 1725. [NRS.CE70.11.1]

ABERCROMBY, ROBERT, second son of Sir Robert Abercromby of Birkbog and Forglen, a Lieutenant of the 93rd Highlanders, was killed at the Battle of Alma in 1854. [AJ.20.9.1854]

ACHTERLONY, DAVID, was buried in St Elisabeth's, Danzig, on 1 January 1628.

ADAM, JAMES, [Jacob Adam], a baptismal witness on 28 March 1632; a Scottish pedlar, father of Maria baptised on 18 February 1634, also his daughter Anna, baptised 3 February 1636, Barbara, baptised on 21 March 1638, James, [Jacob], baptised 4 December 1641, all in Mohrungen.

ADAMS, ROBERT, master of the Ann, bound from Port Glasgow to St Petersburg in 1742. [SHR]

ADAMSON, GEORGE, master of the George of Dundee, trading between Dundee and Konigsberg [Kaliningrad] in 1681. [DSL] [NRS.E72.7.5]

ADAMSON, JOHN, married Elisabeth Cartel in the Burgkirche, Konigsberg, [Kaliningrad] on 1 April 1642.

ADAMSON, WILLIAM, master of the Hopeful Adventure, from Danzig [Gdansk] to Dundee in 1669. [NRS.E72.7.1]

ADOLPHUS, GUSTAVUS, King of Sweden, at Stettin, Pomerania, letters to the Marquis of Hamilton, dated 3 December 1630. [NRS.GD406.1.10449/10451]

AHRENS, Captain J. J., of the Aurora of Bardt, in Prussia, and James Sutherland a merchant in Lerwick, a petition for survey, 1835. [NRS.SC12.6.1835.96]

AIDY, ALEXANDER, son of David Aidy a burgess of Aberdeen, emigrated from Aberdeen to Poland in 1637. [SCM.v.348]; Alexander Aidy and family, were buried in St Peter and Paul's Reformed Church in Danzig [Gdansk] in 1690.

AIKENHEAD, DAVID, a merchant in Tarnow, also in Rzeszow in 1677. [SCA.98]

AIMER, GEORGE, master of the Athol of Perth trading between Riga and Dundee in 1783. [NRS.E504.11.11]

AIR, JOHN, master of the Agnes of Bo'ness, trading with Danzig [now Gdansk] in 1681. [NRS.E72.1.7]

AITKENHEAD, THOMAS, born 1767, died in Riga during 1804. [Arbroath Abbey gravestone]

ALEXANDER, ..., master of the Elizabeth of Aberdeen, arrived from the Baltic in 1710. [CTB.24.293]

ALISON, ALBERT, [Albrecht Aillison], a Scot, married Catherine, daughter of Georg Elsner on 18 October 1644 in St Elisabeth's, Danzig, [Gdansk].

ALISON, WILLIAM, master of the Humphrey of Dundee, trading between Riga and Dundee in 1737, 1738. [NRS.CE52.1.2/3/4]

ALLAN, ALEXANDER, a merchant in Rakow in 1664. [SCA.95]

ALLAN, ANDREW, a merchant in Rakow in 1664. [SCA.95]

ALLAN, EDWARD, a merchant in Rakow in 1664. [SCA.95]

ALLAN, DAVID, master of the Ann of Portsoy, trading between Aberdeen and Danzig [Gdansk] in 1743, 1745; the David of Portsoy, trading between Aberdeen and Danzig [now Gdansk] in 1750. [NRS.E504.1.1/3]

ALLAN, JOHN, master of the James of Queensferry, trading between Leith and Danzig [now Gdansk] in 1691. [NRS.E72.15.44]

ALLAN, ROBERT, master of the James of Dumfries trading between Danzig and Dumfries in1712. [CTB.27ii.0-89]

ALLAN, WILLIAM, in St Petersburg, letter, 1812. [NRS.NRAS.2177.698/706]

ALLASTER, PETER, master of the Well Met of Portsoy, trading between Aberdeen and Danzig [now Gdansk] in 1747. [NRS.E504.1.2]

ANDERSON, ALEXANDER, master of the Christian and Agnes trading between Konigsberg [Kaliningrad] and Dundee in 1773. [NRS.E504.11.8]

ANDERSON, DAVID, in Konigsberg, [Kaliningrad], a letter to the Church of Scotland in 1737. [NRS.CH1.2.75/211-212]

ANDERSON, DAVID, born 1794 in Dundee, died in Riga on 28 September 1834. [Riga gravestone]

ANDERSON, GEORGE, born 1618 in Errol, Perthshire, settled in Kedainiai from 1649 to 1695. [SCL.46]

ANDERSON, JAMES, master of the Hope trading between Konigsberg [Kaliningrad] and Dundee in 1643. [NRS.E72.7.1]

ANDERSON, JOHN, a shipmaster trading between Dundee and Danzig [Gdansk] in 1574. [RAK/STR]

ANDERSON, JOHN, a shipmaster in Aberdeen trading with Danzig [Gdansk] in August 1645. [ASW.287]

ANDERSON, MATTHEW, in St Petersburg, letters, 1812, 1814. [NRS.NRAS.2177.698/706]

ANDERSON, WILLIAM, a Scot, the burgomaster of Augerburg in 1648.

ANGUS, JAMES, master of the Barbara of Leith, trading between Leith and Danzig [now Gdansk] in 1672. [NRS.E72.15.21]

ANSTRUTHER, HENRY, born 4 June 1836, a Lieutenant of the Royal Ulster Fusiliers, died on 20 September 1854 at the Battle of Alma. [St Monance gravestone]

ANSTRUTHER, Colonel, in Konigsberg, [Kaliningrad] four letters, 1796. [NRS.NRAS.3955.60.1.443]

ARBUCKLE, HUGH, a merchant in Queensferry, trading with Memel in 1809. [NRS.CS96.4151]

ARBUTHNOTT, THOMAS, master of the Clementina of Peterhead, trading between Riga and Aberdeen in 1751, 1752. [NRS.E504.1.4]

ARNOT, CHRISTOPHER, son of Albert Arnot, a Scot, and his wife Maria, was baptised in Tilsit [Sovetsk] on 8 July 1668. [Tilsit Reformed Church Records]

ARNOT, JAMES, son of Peter Arnot of Balcormo, Fife, was apprenticed to John Cunningham a goldsmith in Edinburgh on 9 May 1589, later a goldsmith in Schillez, Danzig, [Gdansk], a sasine by 1605. [ERA][NRS. Sasines, Fife.5.6]

ARNOT, JOHN, son of Alexander Arnot of Lochrig, Ayrshire, settled in Kedainiai in 1630s, a birth brief dated 1634, [BL.Egerton Collection], a merchant, died 1678. [SCL.46/246]; with a house on Konska Street, Kedainai Market Square in 1663. [SCA.247]

ARNOT, WILLIAM, son of Peter Arnot of Balcormo, Fife, was apprenticed to George Heriot a goldsmith in Edinburgh on 20 July 1589, later a goldsmith in Schillez, Danzig, [Gdansk], a sasine by 1605. [ERA][NRS.Sasines, Fife.5.6]

ARROTT, WILLIAM, in Konigsberg, [Kaliningrad], son of James Arrott of Inverqueich, a disposition of a bond in favour of his brother Andrew Arrott in 1681. [NRS.GD16.2.98]

AUCHENLECK, [Afflak], ANDREW, a burgher of Sandomierz in 1587. [SCA.95]

AUCHINLECK, JOHN, [Johannes Authimlecius], from Aberdeen, matriculated at the University of Konigsberg, Kaliningrad], in 1580.

AUCHINVALE, THOMAS, born in Drumtrochar near Kilsyth, was granted a birth-brief by the magistrates of Stirling in 1614, probably settled in Elbing, Prussia, and died there on 1653. [SS.35]

AUCHTERLONIE, [Achterlon], CASPER, in Checiny in 1638. [SCA.89]

AULD, ROBERT, master of the Pelican of Saltcoats, a charter party with Daniel Mussenden, a merchant in Belfast, for a voyage to Riga, dated 29 June 1731. [PRONI.D354.395]

AYTOUN, DAVID, an army surgeon, in Stavgard, a letter, 1713, and in Riga, a letter to his brother Roger Aytoun the younger of Inchdairnie, Fife, 1722. [NRS.GD1.42.1.23.6]

BAIK, P. H., master of the Elida of Ny Carleby from Finland was shipwrecked in Lochbuy, Mull, in 1833. [NRS.GD174.1700]

BAILLIE, ALEXANDER, a pedlar in Kedainiai from 1679-1689. [SCL.252]

BAILLIE, D., of the Scottish Brotherhood in Konigsberg in 1701. [SIG]

BAILLIE, THOMAS, master of the Joseph of Dundee, bound for Danzig [Gdansk] in 1721, 1722. [NRS.E508]

BAILLIE, WILLIAM, of Carnbrae, formerly a merchant in Poland versus the executors of Alexander Nisbet, a merchant in Melvinge in Prussia, see letter from the Court of Session in Scotland to the Chancellor of Poland on 24 March 1619. [NRS.RH9.5.34.1]; a testimony as to the transactions between William Baillie and the late Alexander Nisbet, by the Burgomaster and Magistrates of Warsaw, dated 24 July 1619. [NRS.RH9.5.34.6]; a letter from the City of Elbing in Prussia, regarding Catherine, daughter of Alexander Nisbet, wife of Johan Jungschulz the burgomaster of Elbing dated 8 July 1619, [NRS.RH9.5.34.2]; a discharge by Johan Jungschulz if dealings with the late Alexander Nisbet his late father in law, dated 8 July 1619. [NRS.RH9.5.34.3]; a letter from the burgomaster and council of Elbing, at the request of Johan Jungschulz the burgomaster of Elbing, that the inheritance of his wife, daughter of Alexander Nisbet, should be divided equally between the said Johan and Andreas Lankagel, the uncle of his wife. [NRS.RH9.5.34.8]

BALFOUR, JAMES, master of the Alexander of Leith from Leith to Abbo in Finland in 1627. [NRS.AC7.2.17]

BALLINGALL, ROGER, master of the Isobel of Dalgetty, trading between Riga and Montrose in 1750. [NRS.E504.24.2]

BALMAIN, JOHN, a Scottish trader in Kedainiai, Lithuania, between 1633 and 1677. [SCL.46/252]

BALMANNO, DAVID, master of the Swift of Crail, trading between Anstruther and Danzig [now Gdansk] in 1767, and with Memel [now Klaipeda] in 1768; between Memel [Klaipeda] and Dundee in 1767. [NRS.E504.3.4; E504.11.6]

BARCLAY, ALBERT, [Albrecht Barkels?], a Scottish glovemaker, married Elisabeth, daughter of Alexander Bartlet in Aberdeen, in St Elizabeth's, Danzig, [Gdansk] on 29 September 1638.

BARCLAY, DAVID, a merchant in Konigsberg, [now Kaliningrad], letters, 1755,1756,1757. [PRONI.D354. 771/778/797/799/811.]

BARCLAY, GEORGE, master of the Renown of Dysart, trading between Memel [Klaipeda] and Dundee in 1769, 1770, 1772, 1773, and between Viborg and Dundee in 1772. [NRS.E504.11.7/8/9]

BARCLAY, JAMES, born 1617, son of Reverend James Barclay and his wife Bessie Duncan in Drumbled, Aberdeenshire, settled in Memel before 1635, was granted a birth brief by Aberdeen Town Council in 1661. [APB]

BARCLAY, JOHN, master of the Charles of Dundee, trading between Riga and Dundee in 1726, 1728, [NRS.CE70.11.1]; master of the Dundee, trading between Dundee and Riga in 1738. [NRS.CE70.1.2]

BARNET, ALEXANDER, married Elisabeth, widow of Georg Schmied in Heilig Leichman, Danzig, [Gdansk], in 1643.

BARNET, [Bernath], PETER, a trader in Cracow around 1602 to 1605. [SCA.99]

BARR, DAVID, master of the brig Warrener of Saltcoats, bound for Memel [Klaipeda] in 1787. [AJ.2060]

BARR, JOHN, master of the George of Leith, trading between Konigsberg [Kaliningrad] and Leith in 1691. [NRS.E72.15.44]

BARRON, JAMES, master of the Margaret of Dundee which was quarantined in the River Tay on arrival from Russia due to cholera, in July 1831. [MD.117]

BARRY, PATRICK, master of the Unity trading between St Petersburg and Dundee in 1779, and between Riga and Dundee in 1780. [NRS.E504.11.9]

BARTON, THOMAS, a burgher of Tarnow in 1639. [SCA.98]

BARTRUM, THOMAS, a merchant from Pinczow trading in Lvov in 1628. [SCA.93]

BAXTER, DAVID, master of the sloop Peggy of Dundee, from Riga to Dundee in 1796. [NRS.CE70.1.8/4]

BAXTER, WILLIAM, master of the Betty and Mary of Aberdeen, trading between Aberdeen and Danzig [now Gdansk] in 1745, 1746, 1747, 1748. [NRS.E504.1.2]

BEALL, ANDREW, master of the Euphan of Kirkcaldy, trading between Danzig [Gdansk] and Dundee in 1765. [NRS.E504.11.5]; master of the Catherine of Dysart, trading between Memel [Klaipeda] and Dundee in 1772, 1781, 1782, 1783. [NRS.E504.11.7/10/11]

BEATON, DAVID, matriculated at the University of Konigsberg, [Kaliningrad], in 1594.

BEATON, JAMES, married Anna, daughter of the late Peter Clarke, from Amsterdam, in St Elisabeth's, Danzig, [Gdansk], on 26 July 1637.

BEATON, PAUL, Governor of Stettin in 1632.

BEATTY, JAMES, at Balaclava, four letters dated 1855.
[NRS.GD45.8.202]

BEATTIE, PATRICK, master of the Success of Montrose, trading between Riga and Montrose in 1744, 1745.
[NRS.E504.24.1]

BELL, GEORGE, the younger, a merchant trading with Riga around 1750. [NRS.NRAS.363/1]

BELL, …, master of the Peggie of Dumfries trading between Riga and Dumfries in 1751. [AJ.189]

BELL, WILLIAM, master of the Riga Merchant of Dundee trading between Archangel and Dundee in 1794.
[NRS.CE70.1.8/90]

BENNETT, GEORGE, possibly born in Musselburgh in 1615, a merchant and soldier in Kedainiai, from 1650 to 1677. [SCL.46/254]; with a house on Zamkowska Street and store on Kedainai Market Square in 1661. [SCA.247]

BERRY, ANDREW, master of the Dundee, trading between Riga and Montrose in 1748. [NRS.E504.23.1]

BERTRAM, JOHN, was admitted to the Merchant Guild of Konigsberg on 22 September 1684.

BETTS, Captain JAMES, master of the brig Unity of Dundee was lost at sea when bound from Stettin to Dundee in 1841.
[MD.148]

BILLBROUGH, ROBERT, master of the George, trading between Konigsberg [Kaliningrad] and Dundee in 1750.
[NRS.E504.11.2]

BIRNIE, JAMES, sometime secretary to the King of Poland, 16… [NRS.RH15.82.11]

BIRRELL, JOHN, of the Scottish Brotherhood in Konigsberg in 1701. [SIG]

BIRRELL, LAURENCE, of the Scottish Brotherhood in Konigsberg in 1701. [SIG]

BIRSE, ROBERT, master of the <u>Catherine of Montrose,</u> trading between Danzig [Gdansk] and Montrose in 1759. [NRSJ.CE53.1.5]

BISSET, THOMAS, was buried in St Johann's, Danzig, in 1643.

BLACK, ANDREW, [Andreas Niger], from Aberdeen, matriculated at the University of Konigsberg, [Kaliningrad], on 27 September 1568.

BLACK, JAMES, son of James Black, married Anna Chalmers, [Kamers], a widow, in St Elisabeth's, Danzig, [Gdansk], in St Elisabeth's, Danzig, [Gdansk], on 28 November 1633.

BLACK, ROBERT, master of the <u>Providence of Dunbar,</u> trading between Danzig [Gdansk] and Prestonpans in 1686. [NRS.E72.15.14]

BLACK, Captain, of the brig <u>Amelia of Dundee</u> was shored at Narva in November 1843. [MD.157]

BLACKHALL, ALBERT, [Albert Blakal], a member of the Reformed Church in Cracow, paid his tithe to King Charles II in 1651. [SAP.71]

BLACKHALL, JOHN, a pedlar, had his daughter Agnes Blackhall baptised in Mohrungen on 4 August 1642.

BLACKHALL, ROBERT, was admitted as a citizen of Cracow in 1622, husband of Ewa Burnet, with 13 children, members of the Reformed Church in Cracow in 1650s. [SAP.74]

BLACKHALL, THOMAS, married Helena, daughter of the late John Norry, in St Elisabeth's, Danzig, on 19 Octobe1636.

BLAIR, JAMES, a Scottish shipmaster trading between Dieppe, France, and Konigsberg [Kaliningrad] in 1574. [RAK/STR]

BLAIR, THOMAS, master of the Mary trading between Memel [Klaipeda] and Dundee in 1780. [NRS.E504.11.9]

BLAND, HENRY, a merchant in Archangel, in Baillie versus Cairnie, a petition before the High Court of the Admiralty of Scotland in 1716. [NRS.AC9.560]

BLUES, JOHN, a shipmaster of Montrose, Angus, who did on 9 June 1851, uncle of Jane, Margaret, and Rebecca Blues in Tagenrog, Russia. [NRS.S/H.1880]

BLYTHE, WILLIAM, [Wilhelm Bleehe], a Scottish pedlar, married Anna, daughter of Hieronymus Polkan, a servant, in Atstadt, Konigsberg, [Kaliningrad] in 1617.

BLYTH, WILLIAM, master of the Gift of God trading between Danzig [Gdansk] and Dundee in 1615 and 1616. [DSL]

BODEN and SKIRVING, merchants in Edinburgh, trading with Pillau [now Baltiysk] and Memel [now Klaipeda] between 1811 and 1829. [NRS.CS96.3985]

BONNERT, PETER, a Scottish cobbler in Tragheim, Koningsberg, [Kaliningrad], father of a young son who was buried there on 11 December 1639.

BONTHRON, ALEXANDER, master of the St Johnston of Perth, trading with Narva and Riga in 1733. [NRS.CE52.1.3/4]

BONULTIE, ALEXANDER, a shipmaster of Dundee, arrived in Aberdeen in 1608 from Danzig [Gdansk]. [ASW.53]

BOWER, THOMAS, master of the Lyon of Dundee, trading between Konigsberg [Kaliningrad] and Dundee in 1683. [NRS.E72.7.12]

BOWMAN, GEORGE, master of the Elizabeth, trading from St Petersburg and Dundee in 1776. [NRS.CE70.1.6]

BOYACK, JOHN, master of the Charming Nancy trading between Riga and Dundee in 1781, and between St Petersburg and Dundee in 1782. [NRS.E504.11.10]

BOYACK, Captain, master of the Caledonia bound from Riga with a cargo of flax to Dundee in 1847. [MD.167]

BOYCE, PATRICK, master of the Mary Jane trading between Konigsberg [Kaliningrad] and Dundee in 1613. [DSL]

BOYD, THOMAS, master of the Three Sisters of Sunderland, trading between Memel [Klaipeda] and Dundee in 1766, 1767. [NRS.E504.11.6]

BOYTAR, DAVID, master of the Mary and Ann of Dundee trading between Riga and Dundee in 1770, 1771, master of the Nancy of Dundee, trading between Riga and Dundee in 1773, 1774, 1775, 1776,1777, 1779, 1780, trading between St Petersburg and Dundee in 1775, 1783; master of the Concord, trading between Elbing and Dundee in 1784. [NRS.CE70.1.6; E504.11.7/8/9/10/11]

BOYTER, ROBERT, master of the Charming Betty of Anstruther, trading with Danzig [now Gdansk] in 1742, 1743, 1751. [NRS.E504.3.1/4]

BRANDT, DAVID, a Scot, a baptismal wtness in Altstadt, Konigsberg on 12 February 1626.

BRANDT, DAVID, a Scottish sailor in Lastadre, did in Altstadt, Konigsberg on 7 March 1640.

BRANDT, DANIEL, a Scot, married Ursula, daughter of Jacob Carder, in Altstadt, Konigsberg, [Kaliningrad], on 24 August 1608.

BRAND, JAMES, [Jacob Brandt], a Scot, married Anna, the widow of Alexander Frock, in Altstadt, Konigsberg, [Kaliningrad], on 25 July 1604.

BRAND, JACOB, a merchant in Amsterdam, versus the Magistrates of Aberdeen, regarding the wreck of the Heydt van Pajleswaand of Hoorn, bound from Riga to Amsterdam, in a case before the High Court of the Admiralty of Scotland in 1749. [NRS.AC8.709]

BRECHIN, ALEXANDER, son of David Brechin and his wife Elizabeth Duncan in Monifieth, Angus, a traveller in Lumberg, in the Duchy of Pomerania, was granted a birth brief by Dundee Town Council on 13 August 1633. [DCA]

BRIDGES, JOHN, master of the Mary trading between Memel [Klaipeda] and Dundee in 1782. [NRS.E504.11.10]

BRINEN, R. V., and Sons, in Archangel, a client of D. and J.H. Campbell, solicitors in Edinburgh, between 1800 and 1806. [NRS.GD253.212]

BRODIE, ANDREW, master of the Catherine of Dysart, trading between Memel, [Klaipeda], and Montrose in 1771. [NRS.CE53.1.8]; trading between Memel [Klaipeda] and Dundee in 1773, 1774. [NRS.E504.11.8]

BROWN, ALEXANDER, and Company, merchants and manufacturers in Arbroath, trading with Riga, Libau, and St Petersburg, 1819-1820, sederunt book. [NRS.CS96.828]

BROWN, GEORGE, a shipmaster trading between Dundee and Konigsberg [Kaliningrad], and Danzig in 1577, 1578. [RAK/STR]

BROWN, JAMES, a minister in Konigsberg, [Kaliningrad], a letter to the Earl of Leven then in Berlin, dated 13 December 1686. [NRS.GD26.13.369]

BROWN, JAMES, master of the Elizabeth and Anne, trading from Konigsberg, [Kaliningrad], and Dundee in 1750; master of the Peggie of Dundee trading between Riga and Dundee in 1776, 1777, 1784, and between St Petersburg and Dundee in 1783. [NRS.E504.11.2/9/11]

BROWN, JOHN, a Scot, was admitted as a burgess of Poznan, [Posen] in 1587.

BROWN, JOHN, master of the Jonas of Leith was contracted to ship a cargo of salt from Bo'ness to Greifswald and from there to Konigsberg [Kaliningrad] in 1627. [NRS.AC7.2.282]

BROWN, JOHN, a Scottish merchant, married Lydia Eckenhut, on 19 October 1666 in the Burgkirche, Konigsberg.

BROWN, JOHN, master of the Charming Janet of Leith, trading between Perth and Viborg in 1766. [NRS.E504.27.5]

BROWN, JOHN, master of the Katherine of Leith, trading between Prestonpans and Danzig [Gdansk] in 1686. [NRS.E72.21.11]

BROW, JOHN, master of the Lovely Mary trading with Memel in 1791. [NRS.CS96.4493]

BROWN, LAWRENCE, a merchant from Dundee, in St Petersburg in 1803. [NRS.S/H]

BROWN, THOMAS, master of the Jean of Dundee, trading between Riga and Dundee in 1762. [NRS.E504.11.4]; master of the Antelope of Dundee trading between Riga and Dundee in 1773, 1780, 1782, and between St Petersburg and Dundee in1783. [NRS.E504.11.9/10]

BROWN, WILLIAM, master of the Two Brothers of Fraserburgh, trading with Danzig [now Gdansk] in 1749. [NRS.E504.1.3]

BROWN, WILLIAM, master of the Europa of Dysart, trading between Riga and Dundee in 1761. [NRS.E50411.4]

BROWN, ……, master of the Fortune of Irvine from Dublin via Stromness bound for Memel, [Klaipeda], in 1796. [CM.1165]

BROWN, Captain, master of the Isabella bound from Riga with a cargo of grain to Dundee in 1847. [MD.167]

BROWN, Captain, master of the Margaret bound from Riga with a cargo of flax to Dundee in 1847. [MD.167]

BRUCE, ANDREW, master of the Trial of Kinghorn, from the Highlands with a cargo of herring to Danzig, [Gdansk], a petition, 1736. [NRS.AC10.228]

BRUCE, General J. D., in Muscovy, a letter, 1720. [NRS.GD37.328]

BRUCE, PETER, [Peter Brusch], a Scot, and his wife Rachel, were the parents of Anna, who was baptised in St Johann's, Memel, [Klaipeda], on 22 February 1617, godparent was William, a Scot.

BRUCE, ROBERT, master of the Betty trading between Danzig [Gdansk] and Dundee in 1782. [NRS.E504.11.11]

BRUCE, STEPHEN, son of James Bruce and his wife Gilles Will, settled in Prussia before 1612. [DCA.Birthbrief, May 1612]

BRUCE, THOMAS, in Vilnius, Lithuania, 1696-1700. [SC

BRUCE, WILLIAM, [Gulienus Brussius], matriculated at the University of Cracow in 1594. [SCA.95]

BRUCE, ……, master of the Union of Aberdeen trading from Riga to Aberdeen in 1784. [AJ.1901]

BRUCE, Captain, master of the Margaret bound from Riga with a cargo of flax to Dundee in 1847. [MD.167]

BRUCE, BORTHWICK, and Company, of Dunbar, weavers in Konigsberg [Kaliningrad], records, 1824 – 1833. [NRS.CS96.329-330]

BRUHL, Count CHARLES, in Warsaw, letters dated between 1756 and 1763. [NRS.GD157.3288]

BUCHAN, GEORGE, master of the Providence of Aberdeen, trading with Konigsberg [now Kaliningrad] in 1748, 1749, trading with Danzig [now Gdansk] in 1749. [NRS.E504.1.3]

BUCHAN, ….., was buried in St Peter and Paul's Reformed Church in Danzig in 1698.

BUCHANAN, RICHARD D., of the Seaforth Highlanders, ten letters from the Crimea, dated 1855. [NRS.GD1.512.51]

BURNETT, ALEXANDER, letters from Trevor Corry, the British Consul in Danzig, in 1765-1766. [NRS.NRAS.1368.59]

BURNETT, ALEXANDER, of Kemnay, Aberdeenshire, born 1734, for many years Secretary to the Embassy, and for some time Charge d'Affaires at the Court of Prussia, died at Kemnay in 1802. [AJ.30.12.1802]

BURNET, BARTHOLEMEW, and his wife Agnes Rait, and two children, members of the Reformed Church in Cracow in 1650s. [SAP.74]

BURNET, JAMES, master of the James of Leith, trading between Leith and Danzig [Gdansk] in 1681. [NRS.E72.15.21]

BURNETT, JOHN, master of the George of Aberdeen trading between Danzig [Gdansk] and Aberdeen in1681. [NRS.E72.1.4]

BURNET, ROBERT, a trader from Tarnow in the Cracow market in 1649. [SCA.99]

BURNSIDE, JOHN, master of the John of Bo'ness, trading between Danzig [Gdansk] and Leith in 1681. [NRS.E72.15.23/25]

BURNSIDE, WILLIAM, master of the John of Bo'ness, trading between Danzig [Gdansk] and Leith in 1689 [NRS.E72.15.44]

BUTCHART, JAMES, master of the George of Montrose, trading between Konigsberg [Kaliningrad] and Montrose in 1682, 1683, 1684, with Danzig [Gdansk] in 1684, 1685. [NRS.E72.16] [RAK/STR]

BYRES, ROBERT, a merchant in Memel, was admitted as a burgess of Montrose, Angus, on 18 February 1767. [MBR]

CABEL, JAMES, master of the Athole of Perth, trading from Memel [Klaipeda] bound for Dundee in 1773 but quarantined in Inverkeithing. [NRS.CE70.1.6]; trading between St Petersburg and Dundee in 1781, between Memel [Klaipeda] and Dundee in 1783 and 1784. [NRS.E504.11.10/11]

CAITHNESS, GEORGE, master of the Nancy trading between St Petersburg and Dundee in 1782, 1784. [NRS.E504.11.10/11]

CAMERON, CHARLES, architect, drawings of Tsarkoe near St Petersburg, 1792. [NRS.NRAS]

CAMERON, DONALD, a private of the 93rd [Sutherland Highlanders] Regiment, a personal account of events in the Crimea in 1854-1855. [NRS.RH4.141]

CAMERON, ROBERT, from Glasgow, matriculated at the University of Konigsberg [Kaliningrad] in 1580.

CAMPBELL, W., Vice Consul of Stettin, second son of Dr John Campbell in Aberdeen, married Emily Cook, second daughter of

C. J. Cook in Essex late of Madras, India, in the British Vice Consulate in Stettin, Prussia, on 15 August 1854. [W.XVIII.1924]

CARKETTLE, JOHN, married Anna Zander or Alexander, in St Elisabeth's, Danzig, [Gdansk], on 22 October 1640.

CARMICHAEL, ALEXANDER, master of the Blessing, trading between Konigsberg [Kaliningrad] and Dundee in 1644, and of the Unity trading between Konigsberg [Kaliningrad] and Dundee in 1646, 1647, 1648. [DSL]

CARMICHAEL, [nee Forbes], Mrs ANNA, died in 1702. [gravestone in St Martin's, Lutheran Church, in Cracow]

CARMICHAEL, JAMES, [Jacobus Karmichel sr], a member of the Reformed Church in Cracow, paid his tithe to King Charles II in 1651. [SAP.71]; was admitted as a citizen of Cracow in 1625, with his wife Anna Dickson and two children were members of the Reformed Church in Cracow in 1650s. [SAP.74]

CARMICHAEL, JAMES, jr, [Jacobus Karmichel jr] a member of the Reformed Church in Cracow, paid his tithe to King Charles II in 1651. [SAP.71]; was admitted as a citizen of Cracow in 1654, with his wife Sarah Burnet and eight children, were members of the Reformed Church in Cracow in 1650s. [SAP.74]

CARMICHAEL, JAMES, and his family, were buried in St Peter and Paul's Reformed Church in Danzig in 1693.

CARPHIN, ROBERT, at Balaclava, a letter, dated 18 February 1855. [NRS.GD1.895.5]

CARR, EDWARD, a Scot, married Elisabeth, daughter of Wilhelm Durhaus, in Burgkirche, Konigsberg, [Kaliningrad], on 26 June 1638.

CARR, JAMES, a Scottish shipmaster trading between Middelburg in Zealand and Danzig [Gdansk] in 1578. [RAK/STR]

CARSTAIRS, JAMES, a militiaman in Kedainiai, Lithuania, in 1650s. [SCL.46/268]

CARTER, ALBERT, [Albrecht Kurter], a Scot, married Catherine, a housemaid, in Altstadt, Konigsberg, [Kaliningrad] on 23 December 1612.

CATHCART, Lord, the British Ambassador to Russia, letters from St Petersburg between 1771 and 1772. [NRS.NRAS.1368.54]

CHALMER, JOHN, [Johan Kamer], son of Wilhelm Kamer a Scot, was baptised in Tilsit [Sovetsk] on 21 June 1657. [Tilsit Reformed Church Records]

CHALMER, REGINA, daughter of Wilhelm Kamer a Scot, was baptised in Tilsit [Sovetsk] on 2 June 1659, the godmother was Anna, wife of Alexander Ritsch, [Ritchie]. [Tilsit Reformed Church Records]

CHALMER, WILLIAM, [Wilhelm Kahmer], a Scotsman, father of Maria and Regina, who were baptised in October 1653, godparents were Anna, David Barclay's wife, and Catherine, wife of Wilhelm Rehtzrd [William Richard?] [Tilsit [Sovetsk] Reformed Church Records]

CHAMBERS, Reverend ALEXANDER, a student of theology and tutor to the family of Daniel Davidson and his wife Catherine Aidy in Danzig, [Gdansk], minister at Wielkanoc from 1709 until 1715. [SAP.81]

CHAMBERS, JAMES, in Cracow, married Elisabeth Orem, born 1620, in Lucianowice in 1641. [SAP.73]; was admitted as a citizen of Cracow in 1655, with seven children, were members of the Reformed Church in Cracow in 1650s. [SAP.74]

CHAMBERS, [nee Sommer], SUZANNE, died 1720. [gravestone in the Reformed Church at Zychlin near Konin]

CHANCELLOR, THOMAS, an apothecary, possibly from Edinburgh, in Kedainiai, Lithuania, 1653-1666, and in Vilnius 1689-1694. [SCL.269]

CHAPMAN, JAMES, a merchant in Dundee and Memel, a letter, 1770. [NRS.B59.37.9.5]

CHAPMAN, JOHN, a Scottish pedlar in Kedainiai, Lithuania, from 1637 until his death in 1652. [SCL.46/269]

CHARA, [?], AGNETA, daughter of Mathew Chares [?], a burgess of Aberdeen, married Wilhelm Niclaus in St Elizabeth's, Danzig, [Gdansk], on 28 November 1627.

CHARTERIS, JOHN, a merchant in Edinburgh, trading with Riga in 1687, papers. [NRS.GB234.RH15.59]

CHEYNE, SAMUEL, a young man from Nowopole near Tarnow, a student at Cracow Academy, tutor to the family of Wilhelm Torrie, a member of the Reformed Church in Cracow around 1650 to 1653. [SAP.77]

CHIEN, JOHN, master of the Generous Betty of Crail, trading with Danzig [now Gdansk] in 1746, 1747, 1749, 1751, 1760, trading with Libau [now Liepaja] in 1767, and with Konigsberg [now Kaliningrad] in 1771. [NRS.E504.3.2/3/4]; master of the Scotstarvit of Crail, trading between Riga and Dundee in 1765; between Danzig [Gdansk] and Dundee in 1780. [NRS.E504.11.5/9]

CHISHOLM, ALEXANDER, born 1830, son of John Chisholm the schoolmaster of Ardler, Donside, died of cholera in Crimea in 1854. [AJ.22.9.1854]

CHIVAS, JAMES, master of the Margaret of Fraserburgh, trading with Danzig [now Gdansk] in 1747. [NRS.E504.1.2]

CHRISTEN, JOHN NICHOLAS, born 1804, master of the Catherien Charlotte of Riga died on 17 January 1849. [Londonderry Cathedral gravestone]

CHRYSTAL, THOMAS, a shipmaster trading between Dundee and Danzig [Gdansk] in 1575. [RAK/STR]

CHRISTIE, DAVID, in Kedainiai, Lithuania, from 1656 to 1698. [SCL.270]

CHRISTIE, THOMAS, master of the Agatha and Jean of Burntisland, trading with St Petersburg in 1746. [NRS.E504.1.2]; master of the Endeavour of Montrose, trading between Riga and Montrose in 1750, [NRS.E504.24.1]

CLAPPERTON, SAMUEL SPENCE, born 1576 in Coldstream, Berwickshire, son of Reverend John Clapperton and his wife Joanna Spence, a Colonel of Horse under Gustavus Adolphus, late Governor of Finland, died in Womar during 1622. [F.2.40]

CLARK, DAVID, master of the John and David of Arbroath, trading between Riga and Montrose in 1746, [NRS.E504.24.1]

CLARK, DAVID, master of the schooner Commerce bound from Dundee to St Petersburg in April 1817, returned via Memel. [MD.97/99]

CLARK, JAMES, a shipmaster trading between Dundee and the Baltic in 1625 and 1628. [STR]

CLARK, THOMAS, master of the George of Dundee trading between Pillau and Dundee in 1798. [NRS.CE70.1.8]

CLARK, WILLIAM, was buried in St Peter and Paul's Reformed Church in Danzig in 1678.

CLAYHILLS, THOMAS, in Reval, [Tallin] correspondence with Admiral Thomas Gordon, between. 1720 and 1730. [NRS.GD24.1.859]

CLEGHORN, WILLIAM, master of the Janet and Jean of Leith from Leith to St Petersburg in 1735. [NRS.GD24.1854.35]

CLELAND, GEORGE, master of the Jane of Pittenweem, trading with Danzig [now Gdansk] in 1750. [NRS.E504.3.2]

CLELLAND, WILLIAM, a factor, died in Wielkanoc in 1651. [SAP.77]

COCHRANE, Colonel Sir JOHN, in Danzig [Gdansk], a letter, 1649. [NRS.GD220.3.191]

COCKBURN, JAMES, [Jacob Korban], in Tarnow, in Rzeszow in 1628. [SCA.100]

COCKBURN, JOHN, [John Korban], in Tarnow, in Rzeszow in 1628. [SCA.100]

COCKBURN, RICHARD, a shipmaster trading between Dundee and Danzig [Gdansk], in 1574, 1575; trading between Dieppe, France, and Danzig, [Gdansk], in 1574, 1576. [RAK/STR]

COCKBURN, SAMUEL, born around 1574, a Captain of Foot in Swedish service in Livonia in 1606, fought in Russia in 1610, a Major General of the Swedish Army, settled in Finland from 1616 to 1621, was wounded near Riga and died there in December 1621, buried in Abo Minster, Finland. [SIS.30][CFR.253]

COCKBURN, THOMAS, a Scottish shipmaster trading between Nieuwpoort in Flanders and Riga in 1574. [RAK/STR]

COLLINS, EDWARD, son of Edward Collins and his wife Susan, a pupil in Nieuwied, Prussia, letters, 1832-1834. [NRS.G177.1.9]

COLVILLE, ARCHIBALD, witnessed a bond by Colonel John Ruthven in Stettin on 6 May 1631. [NRS.GD26.4.41]

COOK, DAVID, a timberman in Leith, bound for Gotland to buy timber in 1605. [NRS.GD63.74]

COOK, JAMES, [Jakob Kiuk], an innkeeper in Kedainiai, Lithuania, from 1649 to his death in 1688, husband of Margaret Soutar. [SCL.46/271][SCA.235]

COOK, JAMES, master of the <u>Fortune of Prestonpans</u>, trading between Danzig [Gdansk] and Leith in 1672. [NRS.E72.15.12]

COOK, JAMES, in Alstadt, was admitted to the Merchant Guild of Konigsberg in 1677, also was a member of the Scottish Brotherhood in Konigsberg in 1701. [SIG]

COOPER, JAMES, master of the <u>Hellena of Aberdeen</u>, trading with Danzig [now Gdansk] in 1749, 1750. [NRS.E504.1.3]

COOPER, WILLIAM, [Vilhelm Kuper], with a house on Konska Street Kedainiai Market Square in 1663. [SCA.235/247]

CORBET, JAMES, [Jacobus Korbet], a member of the Reformed Church in Cracow, paid his tithe to King Charles II in 1651. [SAP.71/74]

CORDINER, ROBERT, master of the <u>Diligence of Peterhead</u>, trading with Danzig [now Gdansk] in 1747, 1750. [NRS.E504.1.2/3]

CORRIE and ELLIOT, merchants in Danzig, [Gdansk], a letter dated 21 January 1756, [PRONI.D354.782]; dispatched timber aboard the <u>La Fortun de la Mer</u>, master Valentin Stemming, for Bradshaw and Alexander in Belfast, a bill of lading dated 18 April 1759. [PRONI.D354.593]

CORSAR, PETER, master of the <u>Providence of Dundee</u>, trading between Konigsberg [Kaliningrad], and Dundee in 1675, 1676, 1677, 1678, 1680, trading between Trondheim in

Norway and Konigsberg [Kaliningrad] in 1682.
[DSL][NRS.E72.7.9/13][RAK/STR]

COUPAR, G., of the Scottish Brotherhood in Konigsberg in 1701.
[SIG]

COWAN, HARRY, in Danzig, a letter, 16--.
[NRS.NRAS.GD297.116]

COWAN, WILLIAM, son of Thomas Cowan in Edinburgh, a brass-founder in St Petersburg, by 1832. [NRS.S/H]

COUTTS, ALEXANDER, and Company, merchants in Danzig, [Gdansk] versus James Nairn, a merchant in Elie, Fife, in a case before the High Court of the Admiralty of Scotland in 1727. [NRS.AC8.345]

CRAIG, JOHN, from Edinburgh, matriculated at the University of Konigsberg [Kaliningrad] in 1569.

CRAIG, JOHN, from the Lothians, in Greifswald, Prussia, a sasine, 1628. [NRS.RS24.13.267]

CRAIG, JOHN, master of the Molly, from Port Glasgow to Konigsberg [now Kaliningrad] in1738. [SHR]

CRAIGIE, GILBERT, of the Scottish Brotherhood in Konigsberg in 1701. [SIG]

CRAMOND, DAVID, of the Scottish Brotherhood in Konigsberg in 1701. [SIG]

CRAMMOND, JACOB, a student at the Kedainiai Gymnasium from 1685 to1686, later resident in Kedainiai from 1690 to 1709. [SCL.276]

CRAMOND, JOHN, married Ursula, daughter of .... Sauer, in Heilig Leichnam, Danzig, in 1645.

CRAWFORD, ADAIR, MD, physician at the Court of the Grand Duke of Oldenburg in Russia, around 1800. [PRONI.D1700.5.18.15]

CRAWFORD, ANDREW, master of the Euphemia, from Port Glasgow bound for Pillau [now Baltyiysk] and Konigsberg [now Kaliningrad] in 1737. [SHR]

CRAWFORD, [Krefert], BALTHASAR, a Scot, married Regina, widow of Andrew Moller, in Heileger Geist in Danzig [Gdansk] in 1623.

CRAWFORD, EDWARD, bound for Prussia to obtain grain in 1543, with a letter from Mary, Queen of Scots, to King Christian. [NRS.GD149.264.181]

CRAWFORD, JAMES, in Narva, a letter, 1727. [PRONI.D654.B2.124]

CRAWFORD, JOHN, married Catherine, widow of Thomas Gall, in St Elisabeth's, Danzig, [Gdansk], on 24 September 1634.

CRAWFORD, PATRICK, of Auchinames, a merchant in Edinburgh, freighted the Jolly Bachelor, master James Miller, from a voyage from Leith via Banff, Strontian, Holland, Danzig, [Gdansk], Venice, and return, a petition, 1737. [NRS.AC10.261]

CRAWFORD, WILLIAM, master of the Two Brothers of Dundee, trading between Riga and Dundee in 1750; master of the Elizabeth of Dundee, trading between Riga and Dundee in 1769. [NRS.E504.11.2/7]

CREE, JAMES, mate of the Owner's Goodwill, trading from Riga via Stockholm to Arbroath in 1768. [NRS.CE53.1.5]

CRICHTOUN, BALTHASAR, married Anna Severin, in St Bartholemew's, Danzig, [Gdansk], in August 1589.

CRICHTOUN, WILLIAM, [Wilhelm Creathon], married Margaret ...., in St Bartholemew's, Danzig, [Gdansk], on 26 October 1608.

CRIE, THOMAS, a Scot, a baptismal witness in St Elizabeth's, Danzig, on 10 July 1639.

CRIGO, WILLIAM, master of the Providence of Montrose, trading between Konigsberg [Kaliningrad] and Montrose in 1686, [NRS.E72.16.16]

CROW, FRANCIS, of the Scottish Brotherhood in Konigsberg in 1701. [SIG]

CROWN, THOMAS, from Perth, an Admiral of the Royal Navy later an Admiral of the Russian Navy, died in St Petersburg in 1841. [MD.149]

CRUIKSHANK, DAVID, a merchant in Tarnow during the 1620s. [SCA.99]

CRUICKSHANK, ELISABETH, daughter of John Cruickshank, ['Joh. Krugkschanck'], a pedlar and a burgess, married Christoph Maress a burgess, in Mohrungen on 24 November 1675.

CRUICKSHANK, GEORGE, [Georgius Kruckszang], was admitted as a citizen of Cracow in 1646, husband of Susanne Jager, paid his tithe to King Charles II in 1651. [SAP.71]; members of the Reformed Church in Cracow in the 1650s. [SAP.74]

CRUICKSHANK, Mrs, wife of 'G.Krukshank', was buried in St Peter and Paul's Reformed Church in Danzig in 1671.

CRUICKSHANKS and Company, in St Petersburg, 1734, linked with Robert Keith. [NRS.NRAS.61]

CUMMING, FENTON, and Company, merchants in Riga, a letter to John Fergus in Kirkcaldy, dated 21 November 1837. [NRS.GD1.1237.1]

CUNNINGHAM, JAMES, [Jacob Kunningam], son of David and Regina Kunningam, was baptised on 9 February 1631 in St Elizabeth's, Danzig, [Gdansk], godparents were Thomas Dempster and Andrew Morton, Scots.

CUNNINGHAM, JAMES, [Jac. Kuniguen], a Scottish merchant in Muntze, was buried in Tragheim, Konigsberg, [Kaliningrad], on 26 April 1637.

CUNNINGHAM, ROBERT, [Robert Kunigem], a Scot, matriculated at the University of Greifswald in 1649.

CURRIE, JAMES, master of the Janet of Kinghorn, trading between Riga and Dundee in 1769. [NRS.E504.11.7]

CUSTIN, DAVID, a skipper in Leith, and Robert Douglas a merchant burgess of Edinburgh, agreed to a charter party for a voyage from Grangepans to Danzig [Gdansk] and return to Leith, on 15 March 1650. [NRS.RH9.17.32.5]

CUTHBERT, [Kutbernth], ALEXANDER, in Skrzynno in 1651. [SCA.97]

CUTHBERT, ALEXANDER, from Aberdeen, a banker or merchant in Thorn in 1659. [SCL.278]

CUTHBERT, ALEXANDER, in Kedainiai from 1687 until his death in 1739. [SCL.278]

DALGLEISH, JOHN, ['Hans Diglische'], a Scottish pedlar, and Maria a prostitute, parents of a child baptised in Altstadt, Konigsberg, on 30 April 1636.

DALRYMPLE, JOHN, master of the Tabitha trading between St Petersburg and Dundee in 1782. [NRS.E504.11.10]; master of the Tibby of Fraserburgh trading between Fraserburgh and Danzig [Gdansk] in 1784. [AJ.1916]

DALYELL, Lieutenant General THOMAS, bound for Poland, was recommended in a letter to Prince John Radzivill,

Chamberlain of the Grand Duchy of Lithuania, by King Charles II, then in exile in Koln, [Cologne], dated 17 August 1655. Also, similar letters to John Casimor, King of Poland, date 1656, and to Alexis Michaelovitch, Czar of all the Russias. [SRS.Binns pp]

DALYELL, THOMAS, in Muscovy, a Lieutenant General in Russian service, was permitted to return home by Alexis, Tsar of Russia, in 1665. [NRS.GD22.1.195]

DARGIE, JAMES, master of the John and Katherine of Arbroath, trading between Danzig [Gdansk] and Montrose in 1767. [NRS.CE53.1.6]

DAVIDSON, ALEXANDER, a British preacher in Danzig, [Gdansk] married Florentina, daughter of the late George Ernest Remus, in the Reformed Church of Saints Peter and Paul in Danzig [Gdansk] on 14 January 1716.

DAVIDSON, JOHN, in Vilnius, Lithuania from 1633, in Konigsberg after 1655. [SCL]

DAVIDSON, HANS, a Scot, married Elisabeth Gordon in the Burgkirche, Konigsberg, [Kaliningrad, on 6 September 1639.

DAVIDSON, JOHN, with a house on Kedainai market square in 1661. [SCA.235/247]

DAW, ANDREW, master of the Nicolas of Crail bound from the Isle of Lewis with a cargo of herring for Danzig, [Gdansk], Konigsberg, [Kaliningrad], and Gothenburg, a charter party dated 16 July 1678, before the High Court of the Admiralty of Scotland on 20 December 1678. [NRS.AC7.4]

DEANS, JAMES, a merchant in Aberdeen freighted the St Joannes of Konigsberg, [Kaliningrad] master Burgie Thurson, for a voyage from Aberdeen to Danzig [Gdansk] and return to

Aberdeen, a petition before the High Court of the Admiralty of Scotland in 1709. [NRS.AC10.78]

DEAS, JAMES, master of the George of Fisherrow, trading between Prestonpans and Danzig [Gdansk] in 1687. [NRS.E72.21.16]

DEMPSTER, JAMES, a Scot, married Barbara Redau in the Burgkirche of Konigsberg in August 1683.

DEMPSTER, WILLIAM, in Kedainiai, Lithuania, in 1652. [SCL.282]

DE THORAIS, ELIZA, in Moscow, grand-daughter of Thomas Purdie a merchant in Edinburgh, 1855. [NRS.S/H]

DEWAR, DAVID, a Scot, [David Durre], and his wife Margaret, were parents of Barbara, who was baptised in St Johann's, Memel, [Klaipeda], on 2 March 1645, godparents were Hans Emmerich, [John Imrie?], Zander Mittelthon, [Alexander Middleton?], and his wife 'Ale'.

DICK, JOHN, [Hans Dick], a Scot, a baptismal wtness in Altstadt, Konigsberg on 12 February 1626.

DICKSON, ALEXANDER, born 1594 in Cracow, a member of the Reformed Church in Cracow, husband of Elisabeth Krause, was admitted as a citizen of Cracow in 1623, parents of eight children, paid their tithe to King Charles II in 1651. [SAP.71/72/74]

DIXON, ALEXANDER, in Tarnow, trading in Ruthenia in 1640s-1650s. [SCA.99]

DISHINGTON, JAMES, master of the Grace of God, trading between Konigsberg [Kaliningrad] and Dundee in 1643. [DSL]

DOABIE, JAMES, master of the George of Dundee, trading between Konigsberg [Kaliningrad] and Dundee in 1677. [DSL]

DOIG, JOHN, a shipmaster trading between Dundee and Konigsberg [Kaliningrad] in 1578, also with Danzig [Gdansk] in 1578; trading between Broage in France and Konigsberg [Kaliningrad] in 1578. [RAK/STR]

DOIG, JOSEPH, master of the Concord of Perth, trading with Danzig [now Gdansk] in 1754. [NRS.E504.27.5]

DONALDSON, ALEXANDER, married Margareta Hall, widow of James Gey, in St Elisabeth's, Danzig, [Gdansk], on 6 September 1637.

DONALDSON, ANDREW, married Anna, daughter of Peter Seidler, in Heilig Leichnam, Danzig, [Gdansk], in 1648.

DONALDSON, JAMES, master of the brig Thetis of Dundee which had been stranded in the Baltic in December 1840, arrived safely in Dundee on 9 February 1841. [MD.139]

DONALDSON, THOMAS, master of the Margaret and Christian of Pittenweem, trading with Danzig [now Gdansk] in 1743. [NRS.E504.3.1]

DOUGLAS, ALBERT, and his brother John, in Lvov in 1644. [SCA.99]

DOUGLAS, DAVID, master of the Robert of Leith, trading between Danzig [Gdansk] and Leith in 1691. [NRS.E72.15.44]

DOUGLAS, REGINA, a Scotswoman, poor in Elbing, [Elblag], in 1677.

DOUGLAS, JOHN, was ordained as a minister in Stirling in 1606, served as a chaplain to the Scots Brigade in the Netherlands and in the English Reformed Church in Amsterdam, graduated Doctor of Divinity in St Andrews in 1622, moved to Kedainiai in 1637. [SCA.230]

DOUGLAS, ROBERT, a General of the Swedish Army in Germany, son of Patrick Douglas of Standingstone, and his wife Christina Lessels, 1648. [RGS.IX.1995]

DOUGLAS, W., of the Scottish Brotherhood in Konigsberg in 1701. [SIG]

DOUGLAS, Captain, a soldier in Memel in February 1631. [JSM]

DOW, Captain, of the brig Hunter of Dundee was shored at Narva in November 1843. [MD.157]

DOWNIE, JOHN, [Hans Dauni], a Scot, a baptismal witness in St Elizabeth's, Danzig, [Gdansk], on 10 July 1639.

DRUMMOND, Sir DAVID, in Litniouritis in Bohemia, in a letter to the Marquis of Hamilton, reported that Sir David and Major General Leslie had captured Landsberg then marched into Silesia, dated 11 September 1634. [NRS.GD406.1.9336]

DRUMMOND, JOHN, ['Hans Dromment'], a Scot, a baptismal witness in Altstadt, Konigsberg, on 12 February 1626.

DRUMMOND, General WILLIAM, bound for Poland, was recommended in a letter to Prince John Radzivill, Chamberlain of the Grand Duchy of Lithuania, by King Charles II, then in exile in Koln, [Cologne], dated 17 August 1655. [SRS.Binns pp]

DRYSDALE, JOHN, [Hans Dresdel], a Scot, and his wife Anna, were parents of Anna, who was baptised in St Johann's, Memel, [Klaipeda] in January 1617, godparents were Mrs Andr. Koch, and Peter a Scot.

DUFF, JAMES, a merchant in Perth, trading with Archangel, ledger 1846-1848. [NRS.CS96.53]

DUFF, PETER, master of the Nancy trading between Riga and

DUNBAR, ALBERT, in Pinczow in 1630. [SCA.93]

DUNBAR, JOHN, master of the Endeavour of Montrose, trading between Riga and Montrose in 1749. [NRS.E504.24.1]

DUNBAR, PETER, Albert Dunbar's representative in Lvov in 1630. [SCA.93]

DUNBAR, PETER, was buried in St Peter and Paul's Reformed Church in Danzig in 1657.

DUNCAN, ALEXANDER, master of the Jean of Dundee, trading between Konigsberg [Kaliningrad] and Dundee in 1686. [NRS.E72.7.23]

DUNCAN, ANDREW, [Andreas Duncke] a journeyman tailor, married Agneta ... in Schlosskirche, Konigsberg, on 18 May 1631.

DUNCAN, GEORGE, a shipmaster of Dundee, bound for Danzig [Gdansk] in 1626. [STR]

DUNCAN, GEORGE, master of the Diligence of Aberdeen, trading with Danzig [now Gdansk] in 1748, 1749, 1750, 1751,1752, also with Riga in 1751; master of the Alexander and Elizabeth of Aberdeen, trading with Danzig [now Gdansk] in 1749; master of the Nancy of Aberdeen, trading between Danzig [now Gdansk] and Aberdeen in 1751, 1752, and with Riga in 1752. [NRS.E504.1.2/3/4]

DUNCAN, HERCULES, master of the Hercules of Montrose, trading between Konigsberg [Kaliningrad], and Montrose in 1669. [NRS.E72.7.4]

DUNCAN, JAMES, a grain and linen merchant in Dundee, possibly trading with Archangel between 1819 and 1820. [NRS.CS96.1820]

DUNCAN, PETER, in Vilnius from 1655 to 1670, in Kedainiai, Lithuania, from 1672 to 1677, in Vilnius 1681 to 1685. [ECL.283]

DUNCAN, ROBERT, master of the Peggie and Jessie trading between Riga and Dundee in 1768. [NRS.E504.11.6]

DUNCAN, THOMAS, a Scot, married Anna, daughter of Jacob Leske of Danzig, [Gdansk], in St Elizabeth's, Danzig, [Gdansk], on 18 October 1627.

DUNCAN, WILLIAM, master of the Robert trading between Danzig [Gdansk] and Dundee in 1643. [DSL]

DUNCAN, WILLIAM, master of the Nancy of Renfrew, from Port Glasgow bound for Konigsberg [now Kaliningrad], in 1745, 1746. [SHR]

DUNCAN, Captain, master of the barque Duke of Wellington of Dundee, was shipwrecked on the Stronscar in the Gulf of Finland in September 1843. [MD.157]

DUNCAN, Captain, master of the Effort bound from Riga with a cargo of grain to Dundee in 1847. [MD.167]

DURNO, JAMES, the Consul for Prussia, in Warsaw, six letters, 1791. [NRS.NRAS.3955.60.1.163-164]; one to Lord Elgin with Polish news, [NRS.NRAS.3955.60.1.98]; British Consul in Memel, [Klaipeda], a pamphlet, 1807. [PRONI.D562.5482]

DURNO and MOIR, merchants in Memel, trading with James Morrison and Company in Perth, around 1770. [NRS.B59.37.4.13]

DURY, JOHN, born 1596 son of Robert Dury, was educated at the University of Leiden, a Calvinist preacher, minister to the English Company of Merchants in Elbing [Elblag], around 1630. [SLC.129]

DUTTON, THOMAS, master of the Thomas of Leith, trading between Memel [Klaipeda] and Dundee in 1767. [NRS.E504.11.6]

DYKES, Captain, master of the Veracity bound from Riga with a cargo of flax to Dundee in 1847. [MD.167]

DYNN, JOHN, a burgher of Tarnow, in Lvov in 1668. [SCA.99]

'DZANN', ANNA, daughter of Jacob Dzann, a Scot, was baptised in the Reformed Church of Saints Peter and Paul in Danzig [Gdansk] on 11 April 1582.

EDGAR, ROBERT, master of the Success of Montrose, trading between Riga and Montrose in 1743, 1747, 1749, 1750. [NRS.E504.24.1]

EDIE, JAMES, a merchant in Danzig, [Gdansk] disbursed 414 guilders to James Shairp, son of William Shairp of Houston, on 22 July 1680. [NRS.GD30.1379]

ELDER, JOHN, master of the Fame of Dundee trading between Riga and Dundee in 1797. [NRS.CE70.1.8/50, 59]; master of the brig Industry bound from Dundee to Riga in January 1804. [MD.87]

ELER, JOANNES, master of the Noah's Ark of Danzig which was wrecked on the island of Unst in Shetland and looted by the islanders, 1593. [NRS.RH9.5.21]

ELLIOT, THOMAS, master of the Riga Merchant of Dundee, trading between Dundee and Archangel in 1803 and 1804. [DCA.CE70.1.10]

ELMSLIE, URSULA, [Urszula Elmsle], born in Cracow, married .... Elmslie, she was a widow in Cracow in 1651. [SAP.72]

ENGLISH, DAVID, master of the Dispatch of Montrose, trading between Riga and Montrose in 1746. [NRS.E504.24.1]

ERSKINE, CHARLES, master of the St Andrew of Crail, trading with Danzig [now Gdansk] in 1768. [NRS.E504.3.4]

ERSKINE, DAVID, master of the St Andrew of Crail, trading with Memel [now Klaipeda] in 1770. [NRS.E504.3.4]

ERSKINE, ROBERT, MD to the Emperor of Russia, a letter from his mother Christian Dundas, wife of Sir Charles Erskine of Alva, in 1717. [NRS.GD24.2.5.194]; wrote, from Moscow, to the Earl of Mar, a letter dated 20 January 1708. [NRS.GD124.15.773]

EUSEBIUS, MUNIUS, at Prenzlau, formerly at the University of Wittenburg in West Pomerania, a letter dated 20 March 1596. [NRS.RH9.2.179]

FAIRFOUL, JAMES, master of the Euphame of Pittenweem, trading with Danzig [now Gdansk] in 1752. [NRS.E504.3.3]

FAIRWEATHER, GEORGE, master of the Thomas and Elizabeth of Dundee, trading between Danzig [Gdansk] and Dundee in 1754, 1756. [NRS.E504.11.3]

FAIRWEATHER, JAMES, master of the Ann and Isobel, trading between Danzig [Gdansk] and Dundee in 1725, 1726, 1727, [NRS.CE70.11.1]; master of the Success of Dundee, trading between Riga and Dundee in 1750, 1754, 1756. [NRS.E504.11.2/3]

FAIRWEATHER, WILLIAM, master of the Thomas, trading between Dundee and Konigsberg [Kaliningrad] in 1664. [NRS.E72.7.1]

FAIRWEATHER, WILLIAM, the younger, master of the Unity of Dundee, trading between Konigsberg [Kaliningrad] and Dundee in 1691. [NRS.E72.7.24]

FARMER, DAVID, was buried in St Elisabeth's, Danzig, on 21 December 1627.

FARQUHAR, [Farchwar], HENRY, a trader from Tarnow, in Lvov in 1647. [SCA.99]

FARQUHAR, [Farcher], ROBERT, was admitted to the Merchant Guild of Konigsberg on 12 March 1690.

FERGUSON, JOHN, master of the Alexander and Elizabeth of Aberdeen, trading between Danzig [now Gdansk] and Aberdeen in 1751. [NRS.E504.1.4]

FERGUSON, ROBERT, master of the Catherine of Montrose, trading between Narva and Montrose in 1750. [NRS.E504.24.2]

FERRIE, SAMUEL, master of the John, bound for Konigsberg [now Kaliningrad] in 1741. [SHR]

FERRIER, THOMAS, master of the Gift of God of Dundee, trading between Konigsberg [Kaliningrad] and Dundee in 1649. [DSL]

FIDES, ……., [Czycon Fideth], in Ilza in 1668. [SCA.90]

FINDLAY, ALEXANDER, master of the Peggie of Dundee, trading between Riga and Dundee in 1781. [NRS.E504.11.9]

FINDLAY, WILLIAM, [Wilhelm Fiedley], a Scot, married Isabella, widow of William Gibson, in St Marien Kirche, Elbing, [Elblag], on 19 April 1657.

FINLAYSON, JAMES, born 28 August 1772 in Penicuik, Midlothian, son of James Finlayson, a tailor, and his wife Margaret McLairin, a textile machinist in Glasgow, settled in St Petersburg, Russia, around 1815 as master mechanic at the Kolpino Workshops, and finally in Tampere, Finland, around 1820 as a textile manufacturer, returned to Scotland in 1837, died in Edinburgh 1852, buried in Newington, a Quaker.

FINNEY, JAMES, master of the George and William, from Konigsberg [Kaliningrad] with a cargo of rye to Stockholm in 1724. [PRONI.D654.B2.11]; an invoice for a cargo of hemp, herring, bristles, and amber, from Konigsberg [Kaliningrad] to Belfast, in July 1724. [PRONI.D654.B2.14]

FLECK, JAMES, a Scottish shipmaster trading between Dieppe in France and Elbing [Elblag] in 1574. [RAK/STR]

FLEMING, THOMAS, master of the Arbroath Packet, trading between Narva and Montrose in 1771. [NRS.E504.24.3]

FLEMING, WILLIAM, master of the Cornwall, trading between Memel [Klaipeda] and Dundee in 1776. [NRS.E504.11.9]

FODANSZ, HENRY, a merchant in Memel, trading with James Morrison and Company in Perth, a letter, 1769. [NRS.B59.37.9.4]

FORBES, ALEXANDER, a trader from Tarnow in Lvov in 1618. [SCA.99]

FORBES, ALEXANDER, master of the Expedition of Aberdeen, from Riga to Aberdeen in 1742. [NRS.E504.1.1]

FORBES, EVA, a merchant in Cracow, during 1610s. [SAP.76]

FORBES, HENRY, of Tolquon, a soldier in Swedish service, died at Kirkholm, Russia, in 1605. [SIS.49]

FORBES, JAMES, [Jacob], a trader from Tarnow, in Lvov in 1620. [SCA.99]

FORBES, JOHN, in Kedainiai, Lithuania, from 1647 to 1653. [SCL.286]

FORBES, PETER, from Mowney, Aberdeenshire, married Anna Constantia Chambers in Lucianowice in 1668. [SAP.73]

FORBES, PETER, and his family, were buried in St Peter and Paul's Reformed Church in Danzig in 1686.

FORBES, Sir ROBERT, received a letter from the Scottish shipmasters in Danzig, re the proposed convoy from the Baltic, dated 13 April 1706. NRS.GD124.15.353.6]

FORBES, THOMAS, an elder in Wielkanoc and Lucianowice in the 1630s. [SAP.79].

FORBES, WILLIAM, a servant of Thomas Siffart in Skrzynno in 1645. [SCA.97]

FOREMAN, JOHN, master of the Peggie of Dundee, trading between Riga and Dundee in 1780. [NRS.E504.11.9]

FOREMAN, ROBERT, master of the Peggie of Dundee, trading between Riga and Dundee in 1781; trading between Danzig [Gdansk] and Greenock in 1787. [NRS.E504.11.9] [AJ.2078]

FOREMAN, Captain, master of the Cyrus bound from Riga with a cargo of grain to Dundee in 1847. [MD.167]

FORRESTER, ROBERT, a shipmaster of Dundee, bound for the Baltic in 1625. [STR]

FORTUNE, GEORGE, master of the Euphame of Pittenweem, trading with Danzig [now Gdansk] in 1747, 1750. [NRS.E504.3.2/3]

FOWLER, ANDREW, master of the James and Rachel of Leith, a petition re a voyage from Leith via Newcastle to St Petersburg and return, a case before the High Court of the Admiralty of Scotland in 1730. [NRS.AC10.1072]

FRAITER, ABRAHAM, [Abrahamus Frede], a member of the Reformed Church in Cracow, paid their tithe to King Charles II in 1651. [SAP.71]

FRASER, ALEXANDER, master of the Friends Desire of Fraserburgh, trading with Danzig [now Gdansk] in 1747; master of the Clementina of Peterhead, trading between Riga and Aberdeen in 1752. [NRS.E504.1.2/4]

FRASER ANDREW, a merchant in Warsaw in 1613, later in Stockholm in 1616, father of Bernard [Berndt] Fraser, factor for the Duke of Courland in Lubeck in 1646. [SG.XIII.4.23]

FRASER, ANDREW, an elder of Lucianowice in 1631. [SAP.79]

FRASER, ANDREW, [Andrea Frazer], was admitted as a citizen of Cracow in 1625, husband of Susanne Hewitt or

Orem, members of the Reformed Church in Cracow in the 1650s, paid their tithe to King Charles II in 1651. [SAP.71/74]

FRASER, DANIEL, trading between Inverness and Danzig in 1721. [SAP.95]

FRASER, DAVID, master of the Concord of Arbroath, trading between Riga and Dundee in 1743. [NRS.E504.11.1]

FRASER, JAMES, a merchant in Riga, son of John Fraser of Kirkton, a bond, 1744. [NRS.AC11.160]

FRASER, JOHN, master of the Lyon of Dundee, trading between Dundee and Konigsberg [Kaliningrad] in 1681, 1682, [NRS.E72,7.8/9]

FRASER, JOHN, master of the James and Margaret of Dundee, trading between Riga and Dundee in 1762. [NRS.E504.11.4]

FRASER, WILLIAM, of Phopachy, to Sweden around 1656 as an Ensign in Lord Cranston's Regiment in the service of the King of Sweden, later settled in Thorn as a merchant. [SAP.100]

FRISSELL, THOMAS, married Engell, widow of Hans Labisch, in Heilig Leichnam, Danzig, [Gdansk], in 1639.

FRISSELL, THOMAS, married Zanderina, daughter of Alexander Tellmer, in Heilig Leichnam, Danzig, [Gdansk], in 1652.

FULLARTON, DAVID, a shipmaster trading between Montrose and Danzig [Gdansk] in 1575 and 1578. [RAK/STR]

FULLARTON, FREDERICK, [Friedrich Follertuhn], a cobbler, married Gertrud Sevitzki, in Tragheim, Konigsberg, [Kaliningrad], on 14 May 1691.

FULLER, ADAM, was admitted as a Member of the Merchant Guild of Konigsberg on 14 December 1688; was a member of the Scottish Brotherhood in Konigsberg in 1701. [SIG]

FULLER, ALEXANDER, was admitted as a Member of the Merchant Guild of Konigsberg on 12 March 1683.

FULTON, ..., master of the Greyhound of Irvine trading between Konigsberg, [Kaliningrad], and Irvine in 1751. [AJ.196]

FYFFE, ALEXANDER, a Scot, a merchant in Insterburg, married Barbara, widow of Peter Bamert, in Tragheim, Konigsberg [Kaliningrad] on 17 October 1644.

GALBRAITH, GEORGE, a merchant in Edinburgh, the factor in Riga for the Earl of Annandale, a contract, around 1660. [NRS.NRAS.2171.126]

GALBRAITH, [Galbraicht], JOHN, a burgher of Tarnow in the early seventeenth century. [SCA.99]

GALLOWAY, DAVID, was buried in St Elisabeth's, Danzig, on 29 November 1627.

GALLOWAY, JOHN, in Vilnius, Lithuania from 1634 to 1652, a brewer there. [SCL.290]

GARDEAN, ALEXANDER, married Sophie Minskoll a widow, in St Bartholemew's, Danzig, [Gdansk], on 3 January 1600.

GARDEN, DAVID, a shipmaster trading between Dundee and Riga in 1576, and with Konigsberg [Kaliningrad] in 1577. [RAK/STR]

GARDINER, WILLIAM, in Warsaw, a letter, 1796. [NRS.NRAS.3955.60.3.8]

GARDNER, JAMES, a schoolmaster in Camelon, later in Russia, husband of Marion Jenkins in Camelon, a Process of Adherence in 1801, [NRS.CC8.6.1114]; later a Process of Divorce, in 1802. [NRS.CC8.6.1134]

GARDUS, WILLIAM, a Scottish widower, married Anna, widow of Andrew Junst, in Heiliger Geist, Danzig, [Gdansk], in 1641.

GARDYNE, MICHAEL, married Anna Ledal, in St Bartholemew's, Danzig, [Gdansk], on 18 January 1590.

GARTEN, ADAM, a Scot in Keiphof, witnessed a baptism in Tragheim, Konigsberg in April 1639.

GARVIE, ….., daughter of Thomas H. Garvie, was born in Zyaradow near Warsaw, Poland, on 4 May 1885. [S.13051]

GASCOIGNE, CHARLES, a merchant at Carron Wharf, later in Russia, 1807. [NRS.CS96.1327]

GAVIN, DAVID, trading with Konigsberg [Kaliningrad] in 1756. [NRS.NRAS.2238. section 2/6]

GAVIN, WILLIAM, master of the Mercury trading between Memel [Klaipaja] and Dundee in 1772. [NRS.E504.11.8]

GEDDY, BARBARA, daughter of Albert Geddy, a Scot, was baptised in Altstadt, Konigsberg, on 27 December 1598.

GEMMILL, JOHN, a cotton spinner in Glasgow and in Russia, papers, 1795-1854. [NRS.GD1.504]

GERN, FRANCIS, a guild member in Lublin I 1677. [SAP.95]

GERN, PETER, a guild member in Lublin I 1677. [SAP.95]

GIBB, JOHN, master of the Friendship of Bo'ness, trading between La Rochelle and Danzig, [Gdansk], a case before the High Court of the Admiralty of Scotland on 20 January 1686. [NRS.AC7.7]

GIBB, THOMAS, master of the Edinburgh Packet, from Leith to St Petersburg in 1715, in a case, Mill versus Gibb, before the High Court of the Admiralty of Scotland in 1737. [NRS.AC8.542]

GIBSON, ARCHIBALD, a merchant in Danzig, [Gdansk] despatched a cargo aboard the <u>Armstrong,</u> master James Egger, to Daniel Mussenden in Belfast, a letter dated August 1754, [PRONI.D354.752]; a charter party with Christian Hopner, a skipper in Danzig, [Gdansk], master of the <u>Anna Theodora,</u> for a voyage from Danzig to Belfast, subscribed in Danzig on 12 August 1755, witness Jacobus Vierhuff a notary. [PRONI.D354.403]; another charter party dated 12 August 1755, with Martin Haubus a Dutch shipmaster. [PRONI.D354.404]; an invoice issued by Archibald Gibson, merchant in Danzig, for goods sent aboard the <u>William and Mary</u> to Belfast for Daniel Mussenden, dated 7 July 1755. [PRONI.D354.587]

GIBSON, Dr A., in Danzig, [Gdansk], a letter dated 1769. [NRS.GD331.42]

GIBSON, JOHN, [Hans Gibsin], a Scot, married Margareta, daughter of George Linnse [Lindsay?], in Altstadt, Konigsberg, [Kaliningrad], in January 1626.

GIBSON, JOHN, a Scot and a Calvinist, was buried on 20 February 1659 at Fischhausen.

GIBSON, JOHN, from Aberdeen, a poor man in Elbing, [Elblag], in 1695.

GIBSON, JOHN, a merchant in Danzig, [Gdansk], a letter dated 1794. [NRS.GB233/MS3012]

GIBSON, ..., master of the <u>Pearl of Irvine</u> trading between Konigsberg, [Kaliningrad], and Irvine, Ayrshire, in 1751. [AJ.191]

GIBSON, ..., a merchant in Danzig, [Gdansk], a letter from King Stanislaus Augustus in Warsaw, dated 19 September 1763. [NRS.NRAS.208.84]

GIFFORD, [Gifert], AGNES, wife of Thomas Siffert in Skrzynno in 1651. [SCA.97]

GIFFORT, MARGARET, daughter of the late James Giffort in Aberdeen, married Albert Cochrane, [Albr. Kocherim], in St Elisabeth's, Danzig, [Gdansk], in St Elisabeth's, Danzig, [Gdansk], on 25 March 1636.

GIFFORD, [Giffert], THOMAS, a merchant in Szdlowiec between 1639 and 1642. [SCA.97]

GILBERT, ALEXANDER, a shipmaster trading between Montrose and Konigsberg, [Kaliningrad], in 1575, and between Montrose and Danzig, [Gdansk], in 1578. [RAK/STR]

GILBERT, ANDREW, a shipmaster trading between Montrose and Konigsberg, [Kaliningrad], in 1628. [RAK/STR]

GILBERT, DAVID, a merchant in Vilnius from 1644 to 1652, in Konigsberg, [Kaliningrad], from 1655 to 1659, and in Kedainiai from 1659 to 1695. [SCL.294]

GILBERT, ELEAZER, minister to Duke Radziwill and Preacher to the Scots Congregation in Keidainiai, author of 'News from Poland.......', which was published in London in 1641. [SCA.232]

GILBERT, JOHN, a shipmaster trading between Montrose and Danzig [Gdansk] in 1574 and 1579. [DAK/STR]

GILBERT, ROBERT, a merchant in Vilnius, Lithuania, from 1642 until his death in 1655. [SCL.294]

GILCHRIST, ..., master of the Pearl of Irvine trading between, Liverpool and Danzig, [Gdansk], in 1751. [AJ.180]

GILKIESON, ..., master of the Pearl of Irvine, trading between Konigsberg, [Kaliningrad], and Irvine, Ayrshire, in 1752. [AJ.250]

GILLESPIE, JOHN, master of the Two Brothers of Arbroath, trading between Riga and Montrose, Angus, in 1743, [NRS.E504.24.1]

GILMORE, DAVID, born in 1740, late a ropemaker in St Petersburg, died on 12 January 1805. [St Cuthbert's gravestone, Edinburgh]

GLADSTONE, ROBERT, a commission agent in Archangel in 1830s. [NRS.GD268.179]

GLASGOW, JAMES, master of the William and Jean of Irvine, bound from Saltcoats, Ayrshire, to St Petersburg in 1744. [SHR].

GOMM, WILLIAM, in St Petersburg, a letter to Lord Maccartney, dated 17 July 1780. [PRONI.D572.7.59]

GOODSON, THOMAS, master of the Cornwall trading between Memel [Klaipeda] and Dundee in 1777. [NRS.E504.11.8]

GORDON, AGNES, in Sandomierz, 1640. [SCA.95]

GORDON, ALEXANDER, from Aberdeen to Sandomierz in 1603, a trader there in 1614, expelled and died in 1623. [SCA.96]

GORDON, ALEXANDER, a soldier in Russian Service at the Battle of Smolensk in 1634, thereafter a merchant in Kedainiai, Lithuania, from1637 until 1663. [SCL.296]; with premises on Zamkowa Street, Kedainai market square in 1661. [SCA.247]

GORDON, ALEXANDER, a journeyman in Schwankruge, a godparent in Tragheim, Konigsberg, [Kaliningrad], on 30 September 1640.

GORDON, ALEXANDER, a fish curer and merchant in Cromarty, trading with Stettin [Szczecin] between1830 and 1831. [NRS.CS96.4609]

GORDON, FRANCIS, 'Royal British Resident', married Anna, daughter of Hans Wegner, apothecary to the King of Poland, in the Reformed Church of SS Peter and Paul in Danzig [Gdansk] on 2 September 1634.

GORDON, GEORGE, a merchant in Tarnow, trading in Jaroslaw and Lvov around 1634. [SCA.99]

GORDON, GEORGE, was admitted to the Merchant Guild of Konigsberg on 28 April 1677, and a member of the Scottish Brotherhood in Konigsberg in 1701. [SIG]

GORDON, GEORGE, of Riga and Montrose, father of Edward Gordon, born 1844, died at sea on 6 May 1885. [S.13068]

GORDON, ISABELLA, daughter of George Gordon, Marquis of Huntly, and his wife Catherine, the wife of John Andrew, Count Morsztyne the Grand Treasurer of Poland, a birth brief, dated 6 March 1700. [NRS.GD44.46.10]

GORDON, Reverend JAMES, superintendent of the Protestant churches in the city of Samogitia, primary pastor of the city of Kieyden in the Kingdom of Poland, a petition to the General Assembly of the Church of Scotland, dated 1731. [NRS.CH1.2.70]; also, in London in 1730. [SCA.239]

GORDON, JOHN, son of William Gordon of Cottoun, Aberdeenshire, a Captain of the Swedish Army, died in Cracow, Poland, around 1664. [Aberdeen Birth Brief of 4 June 1668, ACA]

GORDON, JOHN, of the Scottish Brotherhood in Konigsberg in 1701. [SIG]

GORDON, KATHERINE, in Poland, a pedigree,16.-7. [NRS.NRAS.1209.59]

GORDON, LOUISA, daughter of the late Francis Gordon, the British Resident in Poland, married John Slater, [Hans Schleter], of the English Nation Society, in St Marien Kirche, Elbing, [Elblag], on 11 February 1659.

GORDON, PATRICK, was appointed Ambassador to Poland and Prussia by King James VI on 2 June 1610. [NRS.GD33.65.5]; an agent in Poland for King James, a bond dated 7 June 1620. [NRS.GD33.17.26]

GORDON, PETER, converted to the Reformed Faith in Cracow during 1640. [SAP.69]

GORDON, PETER, trading in Ruthenia in 1630. [SCA.93]

GORDON, RICHARD, husband of Elisabeth Torrie, with one child, a citizen of Lwow, members of the Reformed Church in Cracow in the 1650s. [SAP.74]

GORDON, ROGER DUFF, son of Lachlan Duff Gordon of Park, died in Riga in December 1806. [Aberdeen Journal, 31.12.1806]

GORDON, THOMAS, Admiral of the Russian Navy, his commission etc, 1691-1741, letter book, 1734-1740, letters 1707-1744. [NRS.GD24.1.854/855/856/857; from Pillau [Baltyiysk] to Danzig [Gdansk] in 1734. [NRS.GD34.1.855/9]

GORDON, WILLIAM, son of Alexander Gordon above, was admitted as a citizen of Sandomierrz in 1624. [SCA.96]

GORDON, WILLIAM, a merchant, a citizen of Checiny between 1631 and 1638. [SCA.89]

GORDON, W., of the Scottish Brotherhood in Konigsberg in 1701. [SIG]

GOURLAY, Mrs JAMES, was buried in St Peter and Paul's Reformed Church in Danzig in 1669.

GOWAN, JAMES, [Jacob Gwond], a Scot, married Eva, widow of Georg Boucke, in St Marien Kirche, Elbing, [Elblag], on 1 March 1661.

GRAEME, DAVID, in Bergen op Zoom, the Netherlands, intended to go to Muscovy, letters to his father Graeme of Braco, Perthshire, in 1735. [NRS.GD220.5.1354]

GRAHAM, JAMES, master of the Peggy of Dysart trading between Memel [Klaipeda] and Dundee in 1771. [NRS.E504.11.7]

GRAHAM, JOHN CHARLES, born 1805 in Danzig, [Gdansk], settled in Charleston, South Carolina, by 1826, and was admitted as a citizen there on 14 May 1829. [NARA.M1183.1]

GRANT, ALEXANDER, a merchant in St Petersburg, a client of D. and J.H. Campbell, solicitors in Edinburgh, between 1800 and 1806. [NRS.GD253.212]

GRANT, FRANCIS, a merchant from Inverness, in Danzig [Gdansk] in 1727. [SAP.95]

GRAY, DAVID, a shipbuilder and shipowner in Kincardine on Forth, with ships trading with Konigsberg, [Kaliningrad], Libau, [Liepaja], and Stettin, [Szczecin], between 1816 and 1821. [NRS.CS96.4205]

GRAY, G. of the Scottish Brotherhood in Konigsberg in 1701. [SIG]

GRAY, JAMES, a member of the council of Kieyden, [Kedainiai], in the Kingdom of Poland, a petition to the General Assembly of the Church of Scotland, dated 1731. [NRS.CH1.2.70]; also, in London in 1730. [SCA.239]

GRAY, ROBERT, master of the Neptune of Dundee trading between Memel [Klaipeda], and Dundee in 1781, [NRS.E504.11.10]

GRAY, THOMAS, master of the Providence of Dundee, trading between Konigsberg, [Kaliningrad], and Dundee in 1664, [DSL]

GRAY, WILLIAM, a Scot, matriculated at the University of Konigsberg [Kaliningrad] in 1603.

GRAY, WILLIAM, of the Scottish Brotherhood in Konigsberg in 1701. [SIG]

GRAY, Captain, master of the Raven from Riga to Dundee in July 1841. [MD.145]

GRAY, Captain, master of the Vera bound from Riga with a cargo of flax to Dundee in 1847. [MD.167]

GREENLAW, JOHN, a spirit dealer in Edinburgh, trading with Russia in 1838. [NRS.CS96.2042]

GREGORY, WILLIAM, master of the Margaret and Mary of Dundee, trading between Perth and Danzig [now Gdansk] in 1749. [NRS.E504.27.3]

GREIG, ALEXANDER, master of the Alexander from Inverness to Danzig [Gdansk] in 1718. [SAP.95]

GREIG, ARCHIBALD, master of the Nelly trading between Memel [Klaipeda] and Dundee in 1782. [NRS.E504.1110]

GREIG, DAVID, master of the Venus of Dundee trading between Riga and Dundee in 1771. [NRS.E504.11.7]

GREIG, THOMAS, master of the St Johnston of Perth, trading between Riga and Dundee in 1764. [NRS.E504.11.4]

GREIG, WILLIAM, master of the Providence of Montrose, trading between Konigsberg [Kaliningrad] and Montrose in 1681, 1683. [NRS.E72.16.1]

GRIEVE, Dr, died in Russia by 1779, a letter. [NRS.GD1.620.134]

'GRIMMESEN, HANS', a Calvinist Scottish youth, died on 22 April 1642. [Altstadt, Konigsberg, church records]

GRUB, [Grube], THOMAS, a Scot, married Catherine, a servant, in Altstadt, Konigsberg, [Kaliningrad], on 19 April 1612.

GUTHRIE, ALEXANDER, a Scot, father of John [Hans Guttlich], who was baptised in Mohrungen on 28 March 1632, the god-father was James Adam a Scot.

GUTHRIE, [Guttry], ALEXANDER, a merchant in Tarnow in 16... [SCA.99]

GUTHRIE, ANNA, was baptised in Jedlinsk on 26 July 1642. [SCA.90]

GUTHRIE, DOROTHY, in Rakow in 1642, mother of Anna [above]. [SCA.95]

GUTHRIE, PETER, in Rakow in 1642, father of Anna, [above]. [SCA.95]

GUTHRIE and BAXTER, merchants in Dundee, between 1836 and 1837 were trading with Archangel, Memel [Klaipeda] and Riga. [NRS.CS96.4738]

HAYD, SIMON, in Rakow in 1633. [SCA.95]

HAIG, JOHN, [Hans Heige], a Scottish soldier, married Dorothea, daughter of Albrecht Moercke a labourer, in Altstadt, Konigsberg, [Kaliningrad], on 20 May 1621.

HALEPEG, JOACHIM, was sent to Scotland by the Hanseatic League to negotiate the return of the St Martin and its cargo, which were captured by pirates, when bound for Revel [Tallinn] in Livonia, then taken to Montrose, a document dated 3 April 1559. [NRS.RH9.5.16]

HALIBURTON, GEORGE, [Jerzy], in Kedainiai around 1659. [SCA.235]

HALL, JOHN, later Sir John Hall of Dunglass, a letter of introduction by the Director General of Posts in Warsaw, to the Master of Posts between Warsaw and Cracow, commanding an adequate supply of post horses for John Hall, dated 15 March 1817. [NRS.GD206.2.324]

HALLIBURTON, ALEXANDER, master of the Heart of Dundee, trading with the Baltic in 1622, 1623. [STR]

HALIBURTON, DAVID, a soldier in Swedish service in Prussia and Poland in 1657, settled in Kedainiai, died in 1668. [SCL.305]

HALLIBURTON, JOHN, master of the John of Perth trading with Konigsberg [Kaliningrad] in 1713. [CTB.27.ii.311]

HALLIDAY, ELIZABETH, youngest daughter of John Halliday in St Petersburg, married Charles J. Baird, from Shotts, Lanarkshire, in St Petersburg on 11 May 1847. [EEC.21511]

HALSON, JOHN, master of the Isabel of Anstruther, trading with Danzig [now Gdansk] in 1742, 1743, 1749, 1761. [NRS.E504.3.1/3/4]

HAMILTON, ALEXANDER, married Sara Classen widow of Hans Jansen, in St Elisabeth's, Danzig, on 21 April 1641.

HAMILTON, ANDREW, a merchant in Prussia and Poland dead by 1655, owner of the lands of Standlawside in Avendale, Lanarkshire, which passed to his brother Archibald Hamilton a merchant burgess of Edinburgh, [RGS.X.374], and in 1664. [NRS.RD2.11.538]

HAMILTON, JAMES, [Jac. Hamelthon], married Margaret Ramsay, in the Burgkirche, Koningsberg, [Kaliningrad], on 8 August 1640]

HAMILTON, JAMES, a merchant in North Leith, and George Gorthie, master of the Isabel of Leith, agreed in a charter party to a trading voyage from Leith to Riga and return, on 30 April 1669. [NRS.RH9.17.32.5]

HAMILTON, JOHN, married Anna, widow of Thomas Kuchel, on 8 February 1645 in the Burgkirche, Konigsberg, [Kaliningad], on 8 February 1645.

HAMILTON, Colonel PATRICK, Commandant of Klaipedia in 1668, later in Piluva 1678-1684. [JSM]

HAMILTON, Marquis of Hamilton, received a letter from King Gustavus Adolphus of Sweden, then in Stettin, [Szczecin], Pomerania, concerning the supply of troops, 2 March 1631. [NRS.GD406.1.10451]

HARPER, WILLIAM, master of the Hunter of Aberdeen trading between Aberdeen and Danzig [Gdansk] in 1672. [NRS.E72.1.3]

HARRISON, ANTHONY, master of the Perth of Shields was contracted via a charter party for a trading voyage from Memel [Klaipeda] to Leith, with John Wardie, a merchant in Edinburgh, on 21 April 1778. [NRS.RH9.17.32.19]

HARVEY, JOHN, [Hans Herwig], from Scotland, married Barbara, daughter of Andreas Muller a linen weaver, in the Reformed Church of Pillau, [Baltyiysk], on 2 August 1654.

HASTIE, ABRAHAM, master of the James of Greenock, from Greenock bound for Danzig [now Gdansk] in 1741. [CM.3374]

HAY, ALEXANDER, a Lieutenant Colonel in Swedish service, with 'a small mansion in the land of Bachman', near Memel, around 1631. [JSM]

HAY, DAVID, master of the John of Dundee, trading between Konigsberg [Kaliningrad] and Dundee in 1657. [DSL]

HAY, FRANCIS, of the Scottish Brotherhood in Konigsberg in 1701. [SIG]

HAY, JOHN, a Scottish pedlar, married Maria, daughter of Hans Lene a tailor, in St Elizabeth's, Danzig, [Gdansk], on 7 February 1627.

HAY, JOHN, master of the John of Leith, trading between Leith and Danzig [Gdansk] in 1681, master of the William of Leith, trading between Konigsberg [Kaliningrad] and Leith in 1681. [NRS.E72.15.21]

HAY, JOHN, master of the Margaret of Arbroath, trading between Danzig [Gdansk] and Montrose in 1749, 1750, [NRS.E504.24.2]

HAY, ISABELL, daughter of Peter Hay the British factor in Stettin, [Szczecin], married Samuel Poulet from Stettin, in Aller Gottes Engel, Danzig, on 15 April 1762.

HAY, PETER, in Kelme, Lithuania between 1711 and the 1730s. [SCL.310]

HAY, ROBERT, master of the Charming Lily of Dundee, trading between Danzig [Gdansk] and Dundee in 1754, and with Riga in 1755, [NRS.E504.11]

HAY, THOMAS, of the Scottish Brotherhood in Konigsberg in 1701. [SIG]

HAY-LEITH, A., a diary of his time in Crimea, 1854. [NRS.GD225.1054]

HAYWARD, Reverend J. H., at Balaclava, a letter dated 1855. [NRS.GD45.8.195]

HENDERSON, ALEXANDER, from Edinburgh, died in Tilsit [Sovetsk] on 20 March 1681. [Tilsit Reformed Church records]

HENDERSON, ALEXANDER, master of the Isabella of Leith, trading between Vyborg, Russia, and Dundee in 1765. [NRS.E504.11.4]

HENDERSON, JAMES, [Jacob], in Lvov and in Lublin in 1620, died 1621. [SCA.100]

HENDERSON, JOHN, master of the John of Prestonpans was contracted at Pillau, [Baltyiysk], Prussia, in August 1629, by Peter Smith, a 'merchant trafficker' in Prussia, to transport goods from Konigsberg [Kaliningrad] to Leith. [NRS.AC7.2.223]

HENDERSON, JOHN, master of the Ossian of Dundee from Memel to Dundee in May 1831. [MD.116]

HENDERSON, THOMAS, master of the Margaret and Euphan of Inverkeithing, trading between St Petersburg and Montrose in 1748, and with Riga in 1750. [NRS.E504.24.2]; master of the Buxton of Dundee, trading between Riga and Montrose in 1748, 1749, between Riga and Dundee in 1749, [NRS.E504.11.1/2]

HENDERSON, WILLIAM, son of James Henderson and his wife Helios Brun, a merchant from Edinburgh, was admitted as a citizen of Cracow in 1600. [SIP.47]

HENDRY, JOHN, master of the Hope of Montrose, bound for Danzig [Gdansk] in 1722, 1723. [NRS.E508]

HENRISON, ROBERT, a Scot, matriculated at the University of Greifswald in 1596.

HERIOT, [Herioth], ANDREW, a burgher of Tarnow in 1602. [SCA.100]

HERVIE, DAVID, was admitted as a Member of the Merchant Guild of Konigsberg on 11 February 1692, was a member of the Scottish Brotherhood in Konigsberg in 1701. [SIG]

HERVIE, THOMAS, was admitted as a Member of the Merchant Guild of Konigsberg on 25 April 1691; a member of the Scottish Brotherhood in Konigsberg in 1701. [SIG]

HERVIE, WILLIAM, was admitted to the Merchant Guild of Konigsberg in 1695, also of the Scottish Brotherhood in Konigsberg in 1701. [SIG]

HERVIE, ..., master of the Unity of Aberdeen trading between Danzig [Gdansk] and Aberdeen in 1755. [AJ.396]

HEWISON, ANNA, [Anna Huysen], member of the Reformed Church in Cracow, in 1651, a merchant in Cracow. [SAP.71/76]

HEWISON, WILLIAM, [Wilhelm Huysen], member of the Reformed Church in Cracow, in 1651. [SAP.71]; husband of Elisabeth Dickson, parents of five children, members of the Reformed Church in Cracow in the 1650s. [SAP.74]

HILL, JOHN, [Hans Hehl], a Scottish pedlar, married Catherine Norman, a widow, in Schlosskirche, Konigsberg, [Kaliningrad] on 22 September 1632.

HILL, JOHN, [Hans Hille], a Scot, from Schlossteich, married Maria Michel, daughter of Daniel Michel the castle carpenter, in Tragheim, Konigsberg, [Kaliningrad], on 12 October 1653.

HILL, WILLIAM, master of the Swallow of Dundee trading between St Petersburg and Dundee in 1770. [NRS.E504.11.7]

HILL, Captain, master of the barque Johns when bound from Archangel to Dundee, was lost in Archangel Bay in 1841. [MD.147]

HODGE, ROBERT, master of the Bachelor trading between Memel [Klaipeda] and Dundee in 1775. [NRS.E504.11.8]

HOGG, JOHN, [Hans Hock], son of William Hogg, [Wilhelm Hock], in Aberdeen, married Maria Moller, widow of Adam Brusse, [Bruce?], in Mewe, banns November 1643, in Gross Nebrau, Elbing, [Elblag].

HOOD, JOHN, [Hans Heyd], a Scot, a baptismal witness in St Elizabeth's, Danzig, [Gdansk], on 10 July 1639.

HOPE, Lord, letters from Poland and Lithuania, 1760. [NRS.NRAS.2171.288]

HORNE, MARGARET, [Margaret Horen], a servant, daughter of ...... Horne, [Horen], from Aberdeen, married John Robertson, [Hans Robertsen], in St Elizabeth's, Danzig, on 27 August 1641.

HOWAT, JAMES, a factor in Archangel, in Hill versus Jaffrey, a petition before the High Court of the Admiralty of Scotland in 1718. [NRS.AC9.474]

HOWIE, DAVID, master of the Lively of Dundee, from Riga to Dundee in 1797, [NRS.CE70.1.8/52]

HUIE, ALEXANDER, master of the Sylvester of Saltcoats, to transport a cargo of flaxseed from Riga to Belfast around 1730. [PRONI.D354.608]

HUNTER, ANDREW, a merchant in Leith, trading with St Petersburg, Memel and Libau in 1770s. [NRS.CS96.1986]

HUNTER, ..., master of the Friendship of Ayr, was shipwrecked on the Pentland Skerries, when bound for Memel [now Klaipeda] in 1787. [AJ.2064]

HUNTER, ANDREW, a merchant in Leith, trading with St Petersburg, Memel, [Klaipeda], Libau, [Liepaja], Archangel, and Riga, from 1774 to 1784. [NRS.CS96.1986/2007]

HUNTER, CASPAR, [Gaspar Huntter], husband of Catherinna, was admitted as a citizen of Cracow in 1651, parents of one child, members of the Reformed Church in Cracow, paid their tithe to King Charles II in 1651. [SAP.71/74]

HUNTER, DAVID, a Scotsman, poor in Elbing, [Elblag], in 1699.

HUNTER, H., of the Scottish Brotherhood in Konigsberg in 1701. [SIG]

HUNTER, JOHN, son of Andrew Hunter, a Scot, was baptised on 25 July 1624 in St Elizabeth's, Danzig, [Gdansk].

HUNTER, THOMAS, in Kedainiai, Lithuania, between 1665 and 1678. [SCL.311]

HUNTER, WILLIAM, trading in Ruthenia in 1628. [SCA.93]

HURST, WILLIAM, master of the Diligence of Kincardine-on-Forth, trading with St Petersburg, Archangel, Vyborg, and Danzig, [Gdansk], 1805-1807. Logbook. [NRS.CS96.3345]

INGLIS, JAMES, a merchant in Edinburgh, trading with Konigsberg, Memel, St Petersburg, and Narva, 1775-1801. [NRS.CS96.2006]

INGLIS, JOHN, a goldsmith in Vilnius, Lithuania, between 1539 and 1546. [SCL.314]

INNES, [Ennies], GEORGE, a merchant in Tarnow in the 1620s, trading in Lvov in 1640s. [SCA.99/100]

INNES, JOHN, in Vilnius, Lithuania, between 1644 and 1650. [SCL.315]

INNES, JOHN, in Opatow, was sued by John Watson a merchant in Lvov in 1671. [SCA.92]

INVERARITY, JAMES, master of the Success of St Andrews, trading between Anstruther and Danzig [now Gdansk] in 1770. [NRS.E504.3.4]

IRELAND, JOHN, master of the Mary of Dundee, trading between Danzig [Gdansk] and Montrose in 1768, [NRS.CE53.1.5]

IRVING, JOHN, a brewer in Langholm, trading with Memel between 1809 to 1813. [NRS.CS96.2048]

IVORY, JAMES, a flax-spinner in Douglastown, Angus, 1799-1803, trading with Marienburg, Druana, Riga, Konigsberg, Libau, Rackitzer, and St Petersburg. [NRS.CS96.3843]

IZAT, ALEXANDER, a shipowner in Kincardine-on-Forth, owner of the Diligence, masters William Hurst and Robert Spittal, trading with St Petersburg, Viborg, Danzig, [Gdansk], and Archangel, between 1805 and 1807. [NRS.CS96.3345]

JAMES, Captain, master of the brig Edenbank of Dundee lost in the Black Sea in 1842 when bound from Constanza to Odessa. [MD.150]

JAMIESON, ELISABETH, daughter of James Jamieson, [Jacob Jacobsen], from Aberdeen, married Wilhelm Moray, a Polish soldier, in St Elizabeth's, Danzig, on 14 September 1627.

JAMIESON, JOHN, master of the Unicorn of Queensferry, trading between Danzig [Gdansk], and Leith in 1691. [NRS.E72.15.44]

JAMIESON, THOMAS, master of the Magdalene of Peterhead, trading between Danzig [now Gdansk] and Aberdeen in 1752. [NRS.E504.1.4]

JANSEN, CORNELIUS, master of the Green Lion of Danzig, [Gdansk], when bound from Langsund in Norway for Naples was captured by Andrew Watson, master of the Blessing of Burntisland, a case before the High Court of the Admiralty of Scotland in 1628. [NRS.AC7.1.218]

JANSEN, EWART, master of the St Peter of Danzig, [Gdansk], was taken at Shetland by Sir John Buchanan the Sheriff of Orkney in 1627. [NRS.AC7.1.48]

JAPP, JAMES, [Jacobus Czap], from Berwick, was admitted as a burgess of Poznan, [Posen], in 1595.

JEFFERSON, FRANCIS, master of the Anne of Whitby, trading between Memel [Klaipeda] and Dundee in 1767, [NRS.E504.11.6]

JOBSON, ROBERT, [Riga Bob], a merchant and agent for the firm of John Jobson and Company in Dundee, in Riga in 1770s.

JOHN CASIMIR, King of Poland, granted a pass to a Scots Colonel in the Polish Army in 1660. [NRS.NRAS.2186]

JOHNSON, AGNETA, daughter of John Johnson, [Hans Janssen], from Dundee, married Georg Dalin a glover, in St Elizabeth's, Danzig, on 27 November 1628.

JOHNSON, NICHOLAS, master of the True Friendship of Hartlepool, trading between Riga and Montrose in 1746. [NRS.E504.24.1]

JOHNSTON, ALEXANDER, a cloth merchant in Danzig in 1647. [NRS.GD190.2.186]

JOHNSTON, JAMES, [Jacob Ianston], trading at the Cracow market in 1617-1618, probably settled in Pinczow between 1633 and 1651. [SCA.93]

JOHNSTON, JAMES, [Jacob Jonston], a burgher of Checiny in 1636. [SCA.89]

JOHNSTON, JAMES, to St Petersburg, a letter, 1834. [NRS.NRAS.3263.11]

JOHNSTON, JOHN, in Kedainiai from 1682 to 1685, then in Vilnius, from 1685 until his death in 1696. [SCL.316]

JOHNSTONE, JOHN, of the Scottish Brotherhood in Konigsberg in 1701. [SIG]

JOHNSTON, JOHN, [Johannes Jonston], a Scotsman from Leifland, a poor man in Elbing, [Elblag], in 1702.

JOHNSTONE, JOHN, master of the Catherine of Dysart trading between Memel [Klaipeda] and Dundee in 1775, 1776, 1777. [NRS.E504.11.8/9]

JOHNSTON, THOMAS, master of the Rebecca of Ayr, a brigantine, a charter party with Daniel Missenden, for a voyage from Aberdeen to Danzig [Gdansk] and from there to Belfast, dated 31 January 1745. [PRONI.D354.402]

JOHNSTONE, Captain, master of the William bound from Riga with a cargo of grain to Dundee in 1847. [MD.167]

JOLLIE, ALEXANDER, master of the Matheson of Montrose, trading between Riga and Montrose in1771, 1773, [NRS.CE53.1.6/8]; and from Riga to Dundee in 1782. [NRS.E504.11.10]

JONES [?], AGNES, daughter of William Jones, [Wilhelm Chons?], a burgess of Aberdeen, married William Marshall, [Wilhelm Morschel], a musketeer, in St Elizabeth's, Danzig, on 21 May 1646.

JORDAN, JOHN, in Kedainia in 16.... [SCA.236]

KAY, DAVID, master of the Nancy, trading between Lipkee, Libau, [Liepaja], in Courland and Dundee in 1777, trading between St Petersburg and Dundee in 1777. [NRS.CE70.1.6; E504.11.8/8/10]

KEAY, MCKENZIE, and MARTIN, merchants in Perth, trading with the Baltic lands from 1845 to 1856 on their ships Rosie and Eagle, [PKA.B59.37.6.1].

KEITH, GEORGE, in Kedainiai, Lithuania, between 1641 and 1653. [SCL.317]

KEITH, JOHN, son of Alexander Keith of Camculter and his wife Margaret Fraser, in Rathen, Aberdeenshire, emigrated to Danzig, [Gdansk], in 1658, was granted a birth brief by Aberdeen Town Council in 1672. [ACA.APB]

KEITH, JOHN, born 1769, a shipmaster in Montrose, died in Riga in 1822. [Craig Inchbrioch, Montrose, gravestone]

KEITH, ROBERT, a Lieutenant of the Kaporski Regiment in the service of Russia, bound for the Siege of Asoph, a letter from Cracow, Poland, 28 April 1736, was in Danzig [Gdansk] on 11 August 1734, other letters from Prussia and Poland in 1738-1739. [NRS.NRAS.61]

KEITH, NATHANIEL, a citizen of Cracow in 1525. [SAP.70]

KEITH, WILLIAM, a trader in Tarnow in 1620s. [SCA.100]

KELLOW, JOHN, [Hans Kylow], a Scot, married Susanna, widow of Heinrich Dahlen, in St Elizabeth's, Danzig, [Gdansk], on 30 January 1632.

KELLIE, JAMES, [Jacob Kelle], from Aberdeen, married Catherine, daughter of Jacob Schmidt of Cassuben, in St Elizabeth's, Danzig, [Gdansk], on 5 July 1638.

KEMPT, GAVIN, a merchant in Leith, trading with Elbing, Danzig, Riga, and Libau, 1785-1787. [NRS.CS96.1061-1062]

KENNEDY, WILLIAM, master of the Isobel and Christian of Dundee, trading between Konigsberg [Kaliningrad] and Dundee in 1764, [NRS. E504.11.5]

KENNERTY, THOMAS, married Jarda, widow of John Farber, in Heiliger Geist, Danzig, [Gdansk], in 1626.

KENNOWIE, EDWARD, in Konigsberg, [Kaliningrad], a letter dated 16 July 1669, and one to his brother John Kennowie in Culross in November 1673. [NRS.GD29.1959.4/6/9]

KENNY, CHARLES, master of the John and David of Arbroath, trading between Riga and Montrose in 1748, 1749, 1750, [NRS.E504.24.1/2]; master of the Ann and Keatty of Arbroath, trading between Riga and Dundee in 1761, [NRS.E504.11.4]

KENNY, WILLIAM, master of the Margaret of Arbroath, trading between Riga and Montrose in 1747, [NRS.E504.24.1]

KERR, JOHN, a merchant in Konigsberg [Kaliningrad] in 1628. [NRS.AC7.2.223]

KERR, WILLIAM, and Son, merchants in Leith, trading with St Petersburg and Riga, in 1822, sederunt book. [NRS.CS96.847]

KETTLEWELL, W., in Narva, a letter to A. Stewart, dated 1726. [PRONI.D654.B2.29]

KEY, JAMES, master of the David of Dundee, trading between Riga and Dundee in 1727, 1731; master of the Elizabeth, trading between Riga and Dundee in 1738; master of the Margaret of Dundee, trading between Riga and Dundee in 1749; master of the Diligence, trading between Danzig [Gdansk] and Dundee in 1750, 1752, with Riga in 1753,1754, 1755,1756 ; master of the Nairn of Dundee, trading between Danzig [now Gdansk] and Aberdeen in 1751, 1752, [NRS.E504.1.4; 11.2] [NRS.CE70.1.1/2][NRS.E504.11.]

KEY, JOHN, master of the Betty and Barbara of Dundee, trading between Riga and Dundee in 1764, 1766, with St Petersburg in 1769, [NRS.E504.11.7]; trading between Perth and Memel [now Klaipeda] in 1767. [NRS.E504.27.5]

KIBBLE, THOMAS, born 1632 in Scotland, served in the Swedish army, settled in Kedainiai and later in Vilnius where he died in 1708. [SCL.317]

KIDD, ALEXANDER, master of the Neptune of Dundee trading between St Petersburg and Dundee in 1771, between Riga and Dundee in 1772, 1773. [NRS.E504.11.7/8]

KIDD, JOHN, master of the Peggie trading between St Petersburg and Dundee in 1780, 1782; and between Konigsberg [Kaliningrad] and Dundee in 1783. [NRS.E504.11.9/10]

KIDD, PETER, a Scott, married Catherine, daughter of Georg Portus, in St Marien Kirche, Elbing, [Elblag], on 6 November 1657.

KIDD, THOMAS, master of the Peggie trading between Riga and Dundee in 1783 [NRS.E504.11.10]

KIER, JOHN, a trader of Tarnow, in Lvov in 1632. [SCA.100]

KINARD, JUDITH, married Valentin Flood, in St Elisabeth's, Danzig, on 24 January 1636.

KING, CATHERINE, widow of William Patterson, died in 1637, members of the Reformed Church in Cracow. [SAP.77]

KING, Lieutenant JAMES, witnessed a bond by Colonel John Ruthven in Stettin [Szczecin] on 6 May 1631. [NRS.GD26.4.41]

KING, ROBERT, [Woyciach Kin], Deacon of the Protestant community of Cracow in 1586.and in 1616 he was senior of Alexandrowice. [SAP.79]

KINLOCH, WILLIAM, master of the Good Fortune of Dundee trading between Poland and Dundee in1616. [DSL]

KINNEAR, THOMAS, master of the Concord of Arbroath, trading between Riga and Dundee in 1746. [NRS.E504.11.1]

KINNERIS, ANDREW, master of the Hope for Grace, trading between Konigsberg [Kaliningrad] and Dundee in 1618. [DSL]

KINNERIS, ANDREW, master of the Hope for Grace, trading between Konigsberg [Kaliningrad] and Dundee in 1639, 1641, 1642. [DSL]

KIRKWOOD, [Kirchwed], WILLIAM, a burgher in Tarnow in early seventeenth century. [SCA.100]

KNIGHT, GEORGE, master of the Jonas trading between Konigsberg [Kaliningrad] and Dundee in1613. [DSL]

KNIGHT, JAMES, a shipmaster trading between Dundee and Danzig [Gdansk] in 1580. [RAK/STR]

KNIGHT, JAMES, master of the Primrose, trading between Riga and Montrose in 1730, [NRS.CE70.1.2]; master of the James of Dundee, trading between Danzig [Gdansk] and

Montrose in 1747; master of the Jean of Montrose, trading between Riga and Montrose in 1748. [NRS.E504.24.1/2]

LAING, FRANCIS, a merchant in Newburgh, Fife, trading with Memel, 1807-1813. [NRS.CS96.1268]

LAING, GILBERT, a merchant in St Petersburg, will dated 1 October 1775. [NRS.GD237.10.15.2]

LAMB, ANDREW, a Scot, married Maria, daughter of Urban Jannen a burgess, banns on 6 April 1638, in Gross Nebrau, Elbing, [Elblag], married in Danzig [Gdansk] on 19 April 1638.

LAMB, ANDREW, a Scot in Nebrau, married Elisabeth, daughter of Albert Monteith, [Albrecht Montje], a Scot in Neumburg, banns, February 1640 in Gross Nebrau, Elbing, [Elblag], married in Neumburg.

LAMB, JAMES, a Scot, father of Anna Lamb, who was baptised in Altstadt, Konigsberg, on 19 June 1600.

LAMB, JOHN, married Helena, daughter of Hans Koning, in Heilig Leichnam, Danzig, [Gdansk], in 1652.

LAMB, ROBERT, a servant of Robert Forbes in Cracow, in 1684. [SAP.77]

LANDEL, ALEXANDER, master of the Concord, trading between Danzig [Gdansk] and Montrose in 1767. [NRS.CE53.1.6]

LANDALE, ANDREW, master of the Andrew and Alexander, trading with Danzig [now Gdansk] in 1744, trading between Riga and Montrose in 1745; master of the Alexander and James of Anstruther, trading between Riga and Montrose in 1745, and between Anstruther and Danzig [now Gdansk] in 1755. [NRS.E504.3.1/3] [NRS.E504.24.1]

LANG, DANIEL, in Kielce from 1614 to 1633. [SCA.91]

LAURENCE, JAMES, [Jacob Laurentz], born 1682 in Scotland, was confirmed in Reichertwalde on 23 October 1701.

LAURIE, ALEXANDER, a journeyman cobbler from Scotland, married Ursula Schwelle, daughter of Hans Schwelle from Radau'schen, in Tragheim, Konigsberg, [Kaliningrad], on 22 November 1643.

LAURY, JOHN, a pedlar, married Margaret Peter Samson, formerly in Swedish military service, in the Burgkirche, Konigsberg, [Kaliningrad]. On 1 May 1647.

LAURIE, WILLIAM, master of the George of Queensferry, trading from Dunbar to Konigsberg [Kaliningrad] in 1627, and returned in March 1628. [NRS.AC7.2.154]

LAW, JAMES, a Scot, married Anna widow of John Hay, in St Elizabeth's, Danzig, [Gdansk] on 23 January 1632.

LAW, WILLIAM, married Christina, widow of Peter Laudin, in St Elisabeth's, Danzig, [Gdansk], on 26 October 1636.

LAW, WILLIAM, master of the Jean and Janet, trading between Riga and Montrose in 1773. [NRS.CE53.1.8]

LAWSON, ALBERT, [Albrecht Lassoen], a Scottish tailor, married Anna, daughter of .... Breuer, in Alstadt, Konigsberg, [Kaliningrad] in February 1631.

LAWSON, BETHIA JANE, daughter of John Lawson in Cairnsmuir, Peebles-shire, died in Moscow, Russia, on 16 January 1899. [S.17341]

LAWSON, JAMES, son of Thomas Lawson, a Scot, was admitted as a burgess of Poznan, [Posen], in 1593.

LAWSON, JOHN, in Kedainiai, Lithuania, in 1637 and 1652. [SCL.318]

LAWSON, ROBERT, master of the Euphame of Pittenweem, trading between Anstruther and Danzig [now Gdansk] in 1752. [NRS.E504.3.3]

LAWSON, [LASSEN], URSULA, a Scot from Mittel Tragheim, and her daughter Anna, were godparents in Tragheim, Konigsberg, on 4 June 1647.

LEE, Captain, master of the Vine bound from Riga with a cargo of grain to Dundee in 1847. [MD.167]

LEISHMAN, [?], WILLIAM, [Wilhelm Litzken], a gentleman from Scotland, a poor man in Elbing, [Elblag], in 1698.

LESLIE, [Lasle], ALEXANDER, in Lvov in 1603. [SCA.92]

LESLIE, Sir ALEXANDER, later Earl of Leven, born 1582 son of George Leslie, a Captain in the Dutch-Spanish War of 1605, a Swedish Army officer from 1608 to 1638, fought in Russia, Colonel of a Swedish Regiment from 1623 to 1629, Major General and Commandant of Stralsund in 1632, in Lower Saxony by 1635, returned to Scotland in 1638, led the Scottish Covenanter Army in its invasion of England in1639, died in Balgonie, Fife, in 1661. [NRS.GD26.3.215-221] [SHR.IX.40] [SIS.41]

LESLIE, ANDREW, in Kedainiai, Lithuania, from 1686 to 1701, a goldsmith. [SCL.320]

LESLIE, EDWARD, master of the Owners Goodwill of Perth trading between Danzig [Gdansk] and Dundee in 1770, 1772, 1773, 1774, and between St Petersburg and Dundee in 1771. [NRS.E504.11.7/8/9]

LESLIE, GEORGE, married Maria Mauben, in St Bartholemew's, Danzig, [Gdansk], on 20 October 1613.

LESLIE, G., of the ScotS Brotherhood in Konigsberg in 1701. [SIG]

LESLIE, JOHN, a journeyman glovemaker, married Elisabeth, daughter of Valtin Muller a mason, in the Burgkirche, Konigsberg, [Kaliningrad], on 9 February 1648.

LESLIE, MARY, a widow, married William Chalmer [Wilhelm Tzammer] in St Elisabeth's, Danzig, on 26 November 1624.

LESLIE, ROBERT, master of the Jean and Ann of Banff, trading between Danzig [now Gdansk] and Aberdeen in 1752, [NRS.E504.1.4]

LESSELS, PATRICK, in Checiny between 1637 and 1647. [SCA.89]

LIDDLE, DAVID, master of the Nancy trading between Konigsberg [Kaliningrad] and Dundee in 1784. [NRS.E504.11.11]

LILLIE, FRANCIS, master of the Hopewell of Inverness trading between Inverness and Danzig, [Gdansk], in a case before the High Court of the Admiralty of Scotland in 1712. [NRS.AC8.145]

LINDER, JOHN, master of the Mary trading between St Petersburg and Dundee in 1783. [NRS.E504.11.10]

LINDSAY, Major ALEXANDER, witnessed a bond by Colonel John Ruthven in Stettin [Szczecin] on 6 May 1631. [NRS.GD26.4.41]

LINDSAY, GEORGE, master of the Constable Galley of Leith, trading between Riga and Dundee in 1769. [NRS.E504.11.7]

LINDSAY, JAMES, a student in Braunsberg in 1596, and at the Jesuit Academy in Vilnius from 1613 to 1614, returned to Scotland, died in 1624. [SCL.320]

LINDSAY, JOHN, [John Lenze], a citizen of Rogozno in 1577. [Warsaw Archive of Old Records]

LITHGOW, JAMES, died in Danzig, [Gdansk] an uncle of Mrs John Brown, according to a letter dated 19 May 1731. [NRS.GD220.5.875.18]

LITHGOW, WILLIAM, a shipmaster trading between Montrose and Stralsund in 1575, 1581, also with Danzig [Gdansk] in 1575, 1579. [RAK/STR]

LITTLEJOHN, ALEXANDER, master of the Wallace and Gardyne, trading between Riga and Montrose in 1771. [NRS.CE53.1.8]

LITTLEJOHN, GEORGE, [Georg Littelson], a Scot and a widower, married Anna, daughter of Hans Hempel, on 21 October 1653 in St Elizabeth's, Danzig, [Gdansk].

LITTLEJOHN, JOHN, [Hans Littelschon], a Scot, and his wife Anna, were parents of Hans who was baptised in St Johann's, Memel, [Klaipeda], on 4 April 1617, godparents were Hans Pesattes, a Scot, [John Bissett?], and Maria, daughter of Henr. Sieber. Resident within the domain of the castle of Memel in 1631. [JSM]

LIVINGSTON, DAVID, a merchant in Lemburg, Poland, heir to his deceased brother Captain John Livingston, son of the deceased Patrick Livingstone of Pitdrichie, 6 April 1727. [NRS.GD1.119.13]

LIVINGSTONE, JOHN, a servant of Robert Forbes in Cracow, in 1694. [SAP.77]

LIVINGSTONE, ROBERT, settled in Kedainiai, Lithuania, in 1664 as a merchant, died in 1701. [SCL.321]

LOCKHART, ALEXANDER, a Scot, married the widow of E. Forbes, in Altstadt, Konigsberg, [Kaliningrad], in 1603.

LONGMUIR, JOHN, master of the Curlew of Aberdeen died in Riga on 19 August 1848. [SG.1744]

LOW, ANDREW, master of the Magalene of Arbroath, trading from Danzig [Gdansk] to Montrose in 1748. [NRS.E504.24.1]

LOW, JOHN, master of the Seaflower of Arbroath, trading between Riga and Montrose in 1749, 1750. [NRS.E504.24.2]

LOW, ROBERT, married Anna Constantia Forbes born 1678, he was Royal Postmaster of Poland from 1695 to 1718, and Royal Secretary from 1713 to 1718. [SAP.73]

LOW, ROBERT, master of the Providence of Aberdeen, trading between Konigsberg [now Kaliningrad] and Aberdeen in 1751. [NRS.E504.1.4]

LOWDEN, THOMAS, a merchant in Holy Spirit Street, Danzig, [Gdansk], died there, inventory, 1629. [Gdansk Archives, 300, R/Vv 190, 29]

LUMSDEN, JOHN, the younger, master of the Theodosia of Aberdeen was shipwrecked off the coast of Sweden when returning from Danzig [Gdansk] in 1741. [NRS.AC9.1472]

LUNAN, ALBERT, a trader from Tarnow, in Lvov in 1647. [SCA.100]

LUNDIE, THOMAS, master of the Robert and John of Anstruther, trading between Anstruther and Danzig [now Gdansk] in 1743. [NRS.E504.3.1]

LYALL, JOHN, [Hans Lewel], a Scot in Walle, was buried in Tragheim, Konigsberg, [Kaliningrad], on 2 July 1651.

LYELL, J., of the Scottish Brotherhood in Konigsberg in 1701. [SIG]

LYALL, ROBERT, in Kedainiai, Lithuania, in 1663. [SCL.324]

LYALL, WILLIAM, in Kedainiai, Lithuania, between 1666 and 1677. [SCL.324]

LYALL, WILLIAM, master of the Christian trading between Danzig [Gdansk] and Dundee in 1784. [NRS.E504.11.11],

LYALL, Captain, master of the smack <u>Active</u> arrived in Dundee on 4 July 1817 in 30 days from Riga. [MD99]

LYON, ANNA, daughter of David Lyon in Edinburgh, married Albrecht Mauritz, in St Elisabeth's, Danzig, [Gdansk], on 12 November 1637.

LYON, PATRICK, from Dundee, married Christina, widow of Johim Ramel, in St Marien Kirche, Elbing, [Elblag], on 26 November 1658.

MAAS, CASPER, master of the <u>Fricade of Danzig,</u> [Gdansk] trading between Danzig and Dundee in 1764. [NRS.E504.11.5]

MCCANDLISH, WILLIAM, Chief Engineer of the Varna Railway, an agreement with Colin Arthur McVean, dated March 1864. [NRS.GD543.2.3.1]

MCCONNELL, Captain JOHN, at Danzig [Gdansk] with a cargo destined for Scotland, a letter dated 17 June 1755. [PRONI.D354.761]

MCDOUGALL, ALEXANDER, born 16 March 1845 in Port Ellen, Islay, emigrated with his father Dugald McDougall to Ontario in 1852, a skipper on the Great Lakes, to St Petersburg in 1875 connected with the development of canals linking the Volga and Don rivers, returned to America by 1886, a shipbuilder and dry dock constructor in Duluth, Minnesota, died May 1823. [HS.21.2/28]

MACFARLANE, ANDREW, a brewer in Vilnius, Lithuania, in 1630s, died 1636. [SCL.325]

MACKAY, ALEXANDER, son of John Mackay and his wife Margaret Munro, a Major of the Swedish Army in Pomerania, died at Strathan-Tongue, Scotland, in 1770. [Book of Mackay.325]

MCKAY, ALEXANDER, master of the Nelly trading between St Petersburg and Dundee in 1780, and between Riga and Dundee in 1781. [NRS.E504.11.10]

MACKEAN, or MACKINNON, JOHN, a tailor in Kedainiai, Lithuania, between 1642 and 1650. [SCL.325]

MACKEAN, JOHN, a skipper in Montrose, trading between Aberdeen and Danzig [Gdansk] in 1633. [ASW.183]

MACKEAN, WILLIAM, [Killianus Makkien], in Bromberg, [Bydgoszcz], in 1615. [SIG.109]

MACKENRICK, DAVID, [David Mackenricht], married Elisabeth, daughter of Martin Drosa a burgess of Neuenburg, were married in St Elizabeth's, Danzig, on 13 June 1627.

MACKENZIE, GEORGE, in Narva, a letter, 1714. [NRS.GD24.1.449]

MACKENZIE, JOHN, master of the Fortrose of Leith, trading between Aberdeen and Konigsberg [now Kaliningrad] in 1749. [NRS.E504.1.3]

MCKENZIE, JOHN, the elder, a merchant and shipowner in Stornaway, trading with Memel [Klaipeda] and Archangel, a letterbook between 1795 and 1836. [NRS.CS96.4475]

MCKENZIE, WILLIAM, was permitted to leave the Russian Life-Guards and return home by Peter, Prince of Courland, on 3 March 1740. [NRS.GD46.6.97A]

MCKENZIE, Mrs, in Archangel, in 1743, mentioned in a letter of George Napier in St Petersburg. [NRS.GD24.2.5.220]

MACKIE, ALEXANDER, a merchant in Aberdeen, trading with Riga and St Petersburg, in 1821, sederunt book. [NRS.CS96.1252]

MACKINNON, or MACKEAN, JOHN, a tailor in Kedainiai, Lithuania, between 1642 and 1650. [SCL.325]

MCLAGAN, Captain, master of the Bellona bound from Riga with a cargo of grain to Dundee in 1847. [MD.167]

MCLAINE, LACHLAN, in Danzig, a letter to Gillean MacLaine, a writer in Mull, dated 10 July 1783. [Gloucestershire Record Office]

MCLAREN, DAVID and WILLIAM, corn merchants in Constitution Street, Leith, a bond of caution for Michael Mitzlaff in Elbing, [Elblag], Prussia, in 1850s. [NRS.SC11.62.4.28],

MCLAREN, MALCOLM, from Glasgow, father of a son born at Novorossisk, the Caucasus, on 20 July 1884. [S.12815]

MCLEA, DUNCAN, in St Petersburg, letters between 1812 and 1821 to Reverend Dr Archibald McLea in Rothesay. [NRS.GD1.456.286]

MCLEAN, ANDREW O'HARA, born 1755 in Mull, Argyll, son of Dr Alexander MacLean and his wife Janet Fraser, an officer of the Russian Amy from 1773, was killed in St Petersburg on 6 December 1812. ['The MacLeans of Sweden', p.39, J. N. M. MacLean, Edinburgh, 1971].

MCLEAN, ARCHIBALD, a merchant in Danzig, [Gdansk], letters to Hector McLean a writer in Edinburgh, dated 1764-1765. [NRS.NRAS.3283.218]

MCLEAN, HECTOR, a merchant in Danzig, [Gdansk], letters, 1764-1765. [NRS.NRAS.3283]

MCLEAN, JOHN, born 1795, died 1867, husband of Eliza Margareta Moir, born 27 April 1805 in Memel, [Klaipeda], died 1873, parents of Eliza born 2 August 1823, died 1911,

Helen born 1824, died 1892, John born 1825, died 1876, MaryAnn, born 1828, died 1865, James, born 1835, died 1865, and Emily, born 1842, died 1919. [Reformed Church in Memel, {Klaipeda.}]

MCLEAN, LACHLAN, a merchant in Danzig, letters from Danzig [Gdansk], and Elbing [Elblag] between 1786 and 1793 to Murdoch McLean of Lochbuy. [NRS.GD174.1398]

MCLEAN, MARIA, from Duart on Mull, was buried in St Salvador's, Danzig, in 1806.

MCLEOD, JOHN, from Inverness aboard the Margaret bound for Danzig, [Gdansk], in 1721. [SAP.95]

MCNEILL, Sir JOHN, a letter book re his voyage to, and the war, in the Crimea, 1855. [NRS.GD1.928.13]

MCNEILL, Sir WILLIAM, a journal of a trip from Tabriz to Kiev in 1828. [NRS.GD371.73]

MCNEIL, JOHN, [John Maknil], a citizen of Kowalewo Pomorski, Poland, in 1577. [SAP.94]

MCPHAILL, WILLIAM, a merchant in Inverness, exporting herring to Danzig, [Gdansk], in a case before the High Court of the Admiralty of Scotland in 1718. [NRS.AC8.215]

MACKQUERSON, GEORGE, son of Alexander Mackquerson, from Torrie, Scotland, married Catherine, daughter of Hans Meden in Neumburg, banns, 1632, Gross Nebrau, Elbing, [Elblag].

MAIDEN, JOHN, master of the Isabella of Dundee, trading between Riga and Dundee in 1763. [NRS.E504.11.4]

MAIDEN, WILLIAM, master of the Virgin of Dundee trading between Dundee and Riga in 1770, 1776. [NRS.E504.11.7/9]

MAINWARING and TAYLOR, merchants in Archangel, a letter to John Drummond of Quarrel a director of the East India Company, in 1711. [NRS.GD24.1.464L]

MAITLAND, JOHN, a Captain in the service of Prince Radziwill, 1660-1677. [SCL.329]

MANSFIELD, ……, master of the Prince William of Saltcoats, from Konigsberg [now Kaliningrad] to Saltcoats in 1753. [AJ.313]

MARJORIBANKS, ANDREW, in Danzig, [Gdansk], a letter, 1679. [PRONI.MIC.19.2]

MARJORIBANKS, EDWARD, in Riga, a letter to M. le Chevalier Stirling in St Petersburg, in 1720. [NRS.GD24.2.5.201]

MARJORIBANKS, GEORGE, died in 'Riga, Sweden', probate, 1685, PCC. [TNA]

MARJORYBANKS and COUTTS, merchants in Danzig, [Gdansk], a letter to Alexander Macintosh of Ternett, Inverness-shire, dated 12 June 1715. [NRS.GD23.6.30]

MARNOCH, ALEXANDER, master of the St John of Aberdeen, trading between Danzig [Gdansk] and Aberdeen in 1682, 1683, 1686. [NES.E72.1.-]

MARR, JOHN, master of the Providence of Dundee, trading between Konigsberg [Kaliningrad] and Dundee in 1681. [NRS.E72.7.6]

MARR, JUSTUS, a Scot, married Regina, daughter of Hans Peters, in Altstadt, Konigsberg, [Kaliningrad], in 1614.

MARSFULLER, MARTIN, tutor to Duke Philip II of Pomerania, son of Bogislaus XIII, wrote to Sir John Maitland of Thirlstane, letter dated Bardi, Pomerania, 11 April 1591. [NRS.GD149.264.230; GD249.2.3]

MARSHALL, A., [Abdr. Marchal], a merchant from Dundee, in Kneiphof in 1692.

MARSHALL, CHRISTINA, daughter of the late Robert Marshall a burgess in Aberdeen, married Lorenz Grehn, on 30 June 1636 in the Reformed Church of St Peter and Paul in Danzig, [Gdansk].

MARSHALL, JOHN, in Kedainiai, Lithuania between 1683 and 1700. [SCL.329]

MARSHALL, THOMAS, was buried in St Peter and Paul's Reformed Church in Danzig, [Gdansk], in 1692.

MASON, JAMES, [Jacob Messunn], from Edinburgh, married Else, daughter of David Watson [Watzum] from Edinburgh, in St Elizabeth's, Danzig, [Gdansk], on 4 August 1633.

MASON, WILLIAM, a shipmaster burgess of Aberdeen, master of the Gift of God trading between Danzig [Gdansk] and Aberdeen in 1596. [ASW.24]

MATHER, JOHN, master of the Jean of Aberdeen trading between Aberdeen and Danzig [Gdansk] in 1683 and 1686. [NRS.E72.1.15/16]

MATHIE, JOHN, master of the John and Elspeth of Prestonpans, trading between Danzig [Gdansk] and Prestonpans in 1685. [NRS.E72.21.10]

MATTHEW, ROBERT, master of the Christian and Ann of Dundee, trading between Riga and Dundee also Montrose in 1750. [NRS.E504.11.2]; master of the James of Dundee, trading between Danzig [Gdansk] and Dundee in 1764. [NRS.E504.11.4]

MAVOR, ROBERT, master of the Thomas and Dorothy of Dundee, trading between Danzig [Gdansk] and Dundee in 1766; master of the Unity trading between St Petersburg and Dundee in 1780, 1781, 1783, also between Riga and Dundee in 1781. [NRS.E504.11.5/8/9]

MAXWELL, JAMES, master of the Phoenix of Dundee, trading between Danzig [Gdansk] and Dundee in 1755. [NRS.E504.11.3]

MAXWELL, PATRICK, a merchant in Edinburgh, bound for Danzig, [Gdansk], was given 264 guilders by Patrick Telfer, a merchant in Edinburgh, to buy goods for delivery to Leith, a case before the High Court of the Admiralty of Scotland on 29 September 1676. [NRS.AC7.4]

MEARNS, Captain, master of the Urania of Dundee, a brig, was shipwrecked when bound from St Petersburg to Greenock in November 1834. [MD.125]

MEIN, Captain JAMES, a Scottish soldier in Kedainiai in 1653. [SCA.238]

MELLING, ELISABETH, daughter of John Melling, [Hans Mehling], from Aberdeen, married George Middleton, [Georg Mittelthon], in St Elizabeth's, Danzig, [Gdansk] on 19 May 1642.

MELNITZKY, ALEXANDER, in the province of Vilna, Russia, a letter-book dating from 1795 to 1802. [NRS.GD1.1063]

MELVEN, JAMES, master of the Betty and Mary of Aberdeen, trading between Aberdeen and Danzig [now Gdansk] in 1748. [NRS.E504.1.2]

MELVILLE, JOHN LESLIE, a traveller in Denmark and Sweden, a letter from St Petersburg on 3 July 1807. [NRS.GD26.13.861]

MELVILLE, WILLIAM, a merchant in Pittenweem, Fife, versus James Melville, a merchant in Pittenweem, and John Haxton, a skipper in Burntisland, re a charter party concerning a voyage to Danzig, [Gdansk], a petition before the High Court of the Admiralty of Scotland in 1729. [NRS.AC10.148/149]

MENNIE, A., of the Scots Brotherhood in Konigsberg,1701 [SIG]

MENZIES, THOMAS, of Balgonie, Aberdeenshire, a Lieutenant Colonel in Russian Service, married Lady Marie Farserson in Riga, father of Thomas Alexander Menzies who died in Riga, John Ludovick, and William; he died in the Ukraine and was buried in Szudna in 1660, a birth brief was granted by Aberdeen Town Council in 1672. [ACA.APB]

MERCER, COLIN, master of the Elizabeth of Dundee, trading between Danzig [Gdansk] and Dundee in 1727. [NRS.CE70.1.2]

MERCER, W., of the Scottish Brotherhood in Konigsberg in 1701. [SIG]

MEPHINE, DAVID, master of the Swift, trading between Prussia and Dundee in 1613. [DSL]

MIDDLETON, JAMES, [Jac. Midelthon], a Scot in Schlossteich, father of William who was baptised in Tragheim, Konigsberg, [Kaliningrad], in April 1639, and buried there on 16 September 1639, also father of Dorothy who was baptised in Tragheim on 30 September 1640.

MILL, D., of the Scottish Brotherhood in Konigsberg in 1701. [SIG]

MILL, JOHN, master of the Lilly of Montrose, trading from Riga to Dundee in 1750. [NRS.E504.11.2]

MILL, [Miel], WILLIAM, a merchant in Sandomierz in 1626. [SCA.96]

MILL, W., of the Scottish Brotherhood in Konigsberg in 1701. [SIG]

MILLER, ANDREW, master of the William of Aberdeen trading between Aberdeen and Danzig [Gdansk] in 1684. [NRS.E72.1.13]

MILLER, BARTHOLEMEW, in Kedainiai, Lithuania, in 1637. [SCL.330]

MILLER, DAVID, of the Scottish Brotherhood in Konigsberg in 1701. [SIG]

MILLER, JAMES, master of the Jolly Bachelor of Kirkcaldy, from Leith to Belfast to Danzig, [Gdansk], to Riga and return to Leith, in a case before the High Court of the Admiralty of Scotland in 1738. [NRS.AC8.574]

MILLER, JAMES, master of the Cumberland, trading between Dundee and Riga in 1750. [NRS.E504.11.2]

MILLER, JAMES, and Company, timber merchants in Leith, trading with Danzig, St Petersburg and Riga, 826-1827, sederunt book. [NRS.CS96.174]

MILLER, WILLIAM, a merchant in Danzig, [Gdansk], was admitted as a burgess and guilds-brother of Glasgow on 1 June 1705, [GBR]; in Vernall versus Barclay, a petition before the High Court of the Admiralty of Scotland in 1714. [NRS.AC9.502]; from Aberdeen, later in Danzig, [Gdansk], in Reid versus Dunn, a case before the High Court of the Admiralty of Scotland in 1720. [NRS.AC9.671]

MILLER, WILLIAM, master of the Speedwell of Irvine, from Port Glasgow to Konigsberg [now Kaliningrad] in 1739. [SHR]

MILLER, WILLIAM, master of the James and Margaret of Dundee, trading between Riga and Dundee in 1760. [NRS.E504.11.4]

MILLN, ALEXANDER, a travelling merchant in Finland, a deed, 10 May 1804, Comm. Moray. [NRS.CC16.9.9/359]

MILLS, JOHN, master of the Unity trading between Memel [Klaipeda] and Dundee in 1783. [NRS.E504.11.11]

MILLS, THOMAS, master of the Sarah of London trading between Riga and London, was shipwrecked near Fraserburgh, Aberdeenshire, in December 1676. [NRS.AC7.6]

MILLS, THOMAS, master of the Blessing of Dundee trading between Konigsberg [Kaliningrad] and Dundee in 1682. [DSL]

MILTON, ALEXANDER, [Alexander Milthon], a burgess of Tranent in Scotland, married Barbara, daughter of Peter Sleinsen of Barlau, Pomerania, banns, 6 February 1662, Gross Nebrau, Elbing, [Elblag].

MITCHELL, ALEXANDER, master of the Neptune of Dundee trading between Memel [Klaipeda] and Dundee in 1783. [NRS.E504.11.11]

MITCHELL, Sir ANDREW, the British Ambassador to Prussia, 1764-1766. [NRS.NRAS.1368.82]

MITCHELL, DANIEL, of the Scottish Brotherhood in Konigsberg in 1701. [SIG]

MITCHELL, JOHN, master of the Cecilia of Arbroath, trading between Konigsberg [Kaliningrad] and Montrose in 1743. [NRS.E504.24.1]

MITCHELL, JOHN, master of the Neptune of Dundee trading between Memel [Klaipeda] and Dundee in 1781. [NRS.E504.11.10]

MITCHELHILL, JAMES, of the Scottish Brotherhood in Konigsberg in 1701. [SIG]

MOBRAY, THOMAS, the Scottish Regimental preacher, married Sara, daughter of the late Thomas Bramston a merchant in Ireland, in St Marien Kirche, Elbing, [Elblag], on 15 July 1659.

MOFFAT, SAMUEL, an officer of the Russian Navy, letters, 1814-1821. [NRS.GD1.1441.1.1]

MOIR, JAMES, in Memel, a petition, 1802. [NRS.CS228.A7.11]

MOLLISON, GEORGE, a resident of Kedainiai around 1659. [SCA.235]

MOLLISON, THOMAS, settled in Kedainiai, Lithuania, in 1633 as a merchant. [SCL.331]

MONCRIEFF, ALEXANDER, a merchant in Kedainiai, Lithuania, between 1672 and 1708. [SCL.334]

MONCUR, HECTOR, [Hector Monga], son of George Moncur [Monga] in Falkirk, married Elisabeth, daughter of William Pattulloch, [Wilhelm Bettillack] in Dundee, banns 7 October 1640, Gross Nebrau, Elbing, [Elblag].

MONTGOMERY, HUGH, a military officer in Radziwill service, 1649-1662. [SCL.335]

MONTGOMERIE, JOHN, born 1701, emigrated to Sweden, in Gothenburg by 1741, husband of Anna Campbell, a factory owner in Sweden and in Finland, died about 1760. [SHR.xxv.294]

MONTGOMERY, …., brother of Captain James Montgomery, in Abo, Finland, in 1763. [NRS.NRAS.3283.371]

MORAY, IAN, in Chmielnik in 1651. [SCA.89]

MORE, DAVID, master of the Expedition of Cellardyke, trading between Anstruther and Danzig [now Gdansk] in 1743. [NRS.E504.3.1]

MORE, JOHN, [Johannes Morre], a Scottish soldier, a poor man in Elbing, [Elblag], in 1681.

MORE, THOMAS, master of the William and Anne of Aberdeen, trading between Danzig [now Gdansk] and Aberdeen in 1742. [NRS.E504.1.1]

MORHAM, JOHN, minister of Colonel Hugh Hamilton's Regiment, matriculated at the University of Greifswald on 22 April 1648.

MORRIS, ANDREW, [Andr. Moritz], born in Scotland in 1578, residing in Stangendorf, was buried at Gross Nebrau, Elbing, [Elblag], on 31 March 1626.

MORRIS, THOMAS, master of the Betsy of Dundee died in St Petersburg in 1839. [MD.134]

MORRISON, ALEXANDER, a letter from Stornaway re a ship arrived from Riga, then in quarantine in 1771. [NRS.GD427.202.27]

MORRISON, ANDREW, [Andreas Moritzen], son of David Morrison, [Moritzen], a Scot, and his wife Anna Robertson, was baptised in St Elizabeth's, Danzig, [Gdansk], on 18 April 1627.

MORISON, JAMES, married Margaret Lenox, in the Burgkirche, Konigsberg, [Kaliningrad], on 16 September 1642.

MORRISON, JOHN, trading in Riga, 1844. [NRS.NRAS.3585.3.3]

MORISON, WILLIAM, married Barbara ....., in St Bartholemew's, Danzig, [Gdansk], in 1597.

MORTON, JOHN, from Tarnow, trading in Ruthenia in 1640s, died a soldier in 1649. [SCA.100]

MORTON, JOHN, [Hans Morten], a Scottish soldier, and Elisabeth, widow of Wilhelm Pomerigs, were married in 1669 in Heiliger Geist, Elbing, [now Elblag].

MORAY, IAN, in Chmielnik in 1651. [SCA.89]

MOUTH?, JOHN, a Scot, married Anna, widow of Wilhelm Artus, in St Elizabeth's, Danzig, [Gdansk], on 2 July 1646.

MOUNSEY, JAMES, in St Petersburg, a physician and chief director of the medicine chancery, a letter, 1762. [NRS.GD24.1.846]

MOUTRAY, [Mutro], ALEXANDER, a servant of Peter Lesels in Szydlowiec around 1645. [SCA.97]

MOWAT, ALEXANDER, executor of the late Alexander Nisbet a merchant in Prussia, in 1619. [NRS.RH9.5.34]

MUDIE, JAMES, master of the James and Peggy of Montrose, trading between Riga and Montrose in 1747. [NRS.E504.24.1]

MUIR, GEORGE, master of the James and Margaret of Dundee, trading between Danzig [Gdansk] and Dundee in 1763. [NRS.E504.11.4]

MUIR, JOHN, master of the Margaret of Leith, trading between Konigsberg [Kaliningrad] and Leith in 1688. [NRS.E72.15.40]; master of the Elizabeth of Leith, trading between Danzig [Gdansk] and Leith in 1691. [NRS.E72.15.44]

MUIR, [Mer], WILLIAM, in Pinczow, trading in Ruthenia in 1631. [SCA.94]

MUIRHEAD, JOHN C. W., father of a daughter born 13 July 1884 in Schouvalova, St Petersburg. [S.12796]

MURDOCH, BALTHAZAR, a Scot, and Lena, a prostitute, parents of Christopher who was baptised in Altstadt, Konigsberg, on 17 February 1639.

MURDOCH, DANIEL, married Catherine Elisabeth, the widow of Joachim Buick, in Heilig Leichnam, Danzig, [Gdansk], in 1638.

MURDOCH, JAMES, son of James Murdoch from Edinburgh, married Catherine, daughter of Andreas Kroppe in Stagendorf, banns, May 1634, Gross Nebrau, Elbing. [Elblag]

MURISON, JOHN, was admitted to the Merchant Guild of Konigsberg on 10 March 1699, also, was of the Scottish Brotherhood in Konigsberg in 1701. [SIG]

MURRAY, JAMES, a courtier at the Polish Royal Court around 1602, in 1609 he was an envoy in Poland for King James, King Sigismund of Poland appointed him as the senior naval architect in Poland in 1620, his first ship was the Yellow Lion built at Puck on the Bay of Danzig, several other ships followed such as the King David of which he was commander at the Battle of Oliwa in 1627. Later he served as a Polish Army captain at the Siege of Smolensk and he became colonel of dragoons against the Russians. [HS.IX.3]

MURRAY, JAMES, a goldsmith in Vilnius, Lithuania, from 1626 until his death in 1634. [SCL.336]

MURRAY, RICHARD, a trader at the Rzeszow Fair in 1650. [SCA.92]

MURRAY, THOMAS, was buried in St Peter and Paul's Reformed Church in Danzig [Gdansk] in 1690.

MUSTART, WILLIAM, mate of the sloop Isabella of Dundee, from Riga to Dundee in 1796. [NRS.CE70.1.8/4]

MYLES, DAVID, master of the Countess of Dumfries of Dundee, trading with Riga in 1753; master of the Peter and Betty of Newburgh, trading with Danzig [now Gdansk] in 1755; master of the Unity trading between Riga and Dundee in 1776, 1777, 1783; master of the Unity trading between St Petersburg in 1777. [NRS.E504.27.3; E504.11.10/11]

NAIRN, ALEXANDER, a Scottish lieutenant, married Dorothea Elschmer a widow, in St Elizabeth's, Danzig, [Gdansk], on 26 February 1647.

NAIRN, [Nern], DAVID, from 'Aberstinensi', in Scotland, in Szydlow, died 1639, father of Sophia and John. [SCA.97]

NAIRN, JOHN, master of the Venus of Dundee, trading between Riga and Dundee in 1764, 1768, 1771. [NRS.E504.11.6/7/8]

NAPIER, Lord FRANCIS, Ambassador in St Petersburg in 1864. [NRS.NRAS.156.5.19]

NAPIER. GEORGE, a merchant in St Petersburg, a letter to his brother James Napier of Ballikinrain, in 1732, a letter in 1743. [NRS.GD1.850.31/37]; a letter to Sir Henry Stirling in Edinburgh in 1743. [NRS.GD24.2.5.220]

NAPIER, WILLIAM, master of the Marjory and Ann of Montrose, trading between Riga and Montrose in 1747, [NRS.E504.24.1] on 17 January 1844. [MD.158]

NEISH, CHARLES, a merchant in Arbroath, versus Trompowsky and Company merchant in Riga, 17 January 1811. [NRS.CS36.1.12]

NEISH and SMART, merchants in Dundee, trading with Riga and St Petersburg, 1826-1827. [NRS.CS96.3731]

NESS, WILLIAM, master of the Catherine of Dysart trading between Memel [Klaipeda] and Dysart in 1774. [NRS.E504.11.8]

NEWLANDS, ALBERT, a pedlar in Kedainiai, Lithuania, in 1637. [SCL.338]

NEWLANDS, REGINA, in Kedainiai, Lithuania, in 1652. [SCL.337]

NICHOLAS, ALEXANDER, a doctor of theology, a lecturer at the College of Kedainiai in 1629. [SCA.229]

NICOL, ALEXANDER, master of the Euphan of Perth, trading with Riga in 1750. [NRS.E504.27.3]

NICOLL.JOHN, a pedlar in Kedainiai, Lithuania, between 1637 and 1664. [SCL.338]

NICOLL, JOHN, master of the America Planter trading between Memel [Klaipeda] and Dundee in 1774. [NRS.E504.11.8]

NICOLL, Captain, master of the Antelope trading between Danzig and Dundee in 1817. [MD.99]

NICOLSON, JOHN, a shipmaster in Fittie, master of the Patience of Aberdeen trading between Danzig [Gdansk] and Aberdeen in 1668, 1669, 1670. [ASW][NRS.E72.1.3]

NIMMO, JAMES, master of the Peggy of Bo'ness trading with Memel, Kronstadt, Konigsberg, Pilau, and Danzig, between, 1763 and 1773. [NRS.CS96.1914]

NISBET, ALEXANDER, a merchant in Mewe [Melving], in the Duchy of Prussia, dead by 1619. [NRS.RH9.5.34]

NISBET, GEORGE, executor of the late Alexander Nisbet a merchant in Prussia, in 1619. [NRS.RH9.5.34]

NISH, WILLIAM, master of the Concord, trading between Riga and Dundee in 1780, 1781, 1782, 1783, trading between St Petersburg and Dundee in 1782, 1783. [NRS.E504.11.9/10/11]

NORMAND, JAMES, master of the Europa of Dysart, trading between Riga and Dundee in 1762, 1763, 1764. [NRS.E504.11.3/4]

NORMAND, MATTHEW, master of the Europa of Dysart, trading between Konigsberg [Kaliningrad] and Dundee in 1763, [NRS.E504.11.4]; master of the Christian of Dysart, trading between Perth and Riga in 1767. [NRS.E504.27.5]

NUCATOR, PETER, master of the Patience, from Memel, [Klaipeda], to Dundee in 1794. [NRS.CE70.1.8/83]

OCHTERLONY, WILLIAM, master of the Lyon of Montrose, trading from Riga to Montrose in 1743. [NRS.E504.24.1]

OGILVIE, ANDREW, master of the Olive from Memel to Dundee in June 1819. [MD.101]

OGILVIE, DAVID, master of the Isabel of Montrose, trading between Riga and Montrose in 1741. [NRS.CE53.1.3]

OGILVY, G., in Memel, a letter to Lord Ogilvy dated 6 July 1631. [NRS.GD16.34.11]

OGILVIE, JAMES, a merchant in Vilnius, Lithuania, from 1633 to 1655, in Slutsk from 1645 to 1651, and in Kedainiai, Lithuania, from 1661 to 1665. [SCL.340]

OGILVIE, JOHN, [Hans Oggelvi], a Scot, father of David Oggelvi, baptised in Altstadt, Konigsberg, on 12 February 1626.

OGILVIE, JOHAN GOTTFRIED, born 19 March 1740 in 'Prussian Holland', died 6 November 1784 in Memel, [Klaipeda], husband of Dorothea Muttray, born 23 May 1750 in Memel, died 21 January 1801 in Memel.

OGILVIE, JOHN, born 9 August 1772, died 18 March 1849 in Memel, [Klaipeda], husband of Susanne Stern, parents of Thomas born 1800, Jacob born 1802, Amanda born 1804, Freidrich born1806, etc .

OGILVY, PATRICK, master of the Friendship of Montrose, trading between Riga and Montrose in 1743; master of the Two Brothers of Dundee, trading between Danzig [Gdansk] and Dundee in 1756. [NRS.E504.24.1; E504.11.3]

OGILVIE, THOMAS, master of the Hope for Grace, trading between Konigsberg [Kaliningrad] and Dundee in 1642. [DSL]

OGILVIE, THOMAS, and JOHN, merchants in Memel, [Klaipeda], a letter dated 3 October 1786. [PRONI.D2651.2.197]

OGILVIE, [Oggelbey], Captain, a soldier in Memel in February 1631. [JSM]

OLIPHANT, [Olefant], ARCHIBALD, a merchant in Tarnow, in Lvov in 1618. [SCA.100]

OLIPHANT, JOHN, master of the Alison of Dundee, trading with Danzig [now Gdansk] in 1745. [NRS.E504.3.1]

OLIPHANT, WILLIAM, a trader in Kedainiai, Lithuania, from 1637 to 1646. [SCL.341]

OMAND, JAMES, master of the True Love trading between Riga and Dundee in 1781, also St Petersburg and Dundee in 1781. [NRS.E504.11.9]

OREM, PETER, son of Thomas Orem, a burgess of Cracow, and his wife Susanne Hewitt, was baptised in Cracow in 1610. [SAP.66]

OREM, THOMAS, a burgess and merchant of Cracow, married Susanne Hewitt, [Zuzanna Heidowna], in Wielkanoc in 1606. [SAP.73]

OREM, or ELMSLIE, URSULA, born 1588, a merchant in Cracow, died 1651. [SAP.76]

ORKNEY, JAMES, master of the Elizabeth of Montrose, trading between Riga and Montrose in 1747, 1749, 1750. [NRS.E504.24.2]

OSTEREUND, Captain JOHN, born 1766 in Helsingford, Finland, a resident of Leith in 1808. [EBR.SL115]

OUCHTERLONY, ..., in Riga, correspondence with Admiral Thomas Gordon, between 1720 and 1730. [NRS.GD24.1.859]

PAIP, ALEXANDER, son of Gilbert Paip of Muckle Rainy, Tain, and his wife Anne Munro, a merchant and guild member in Lublin from 1668, moved to Danzig [Gdansk] in the 1680s, father of Alexander, was buried in St Peter and St Paul's church there. [SAP.95/96]

PAIP, GEORGE, a court servitor and wholesaler on Market Square, Warsaw, in 1700. [SAP.96]

PANTON, H., of the Scottish Brotherhood in Konigsberg in 1701. [SIG]

PARIS, ROBERT, mate of the Peggy of Dundee, trading between Riga and Dundee in 1796. [NRS.CE70.1.8/4]

PARK, THOMAS, master of the Friendship of Peterhead, trading between Danzig [now Gdansk] and Aberdeen in 1752. [NRS.E504.1.4]

PATERSON, [nee King], CATHERINE, died 1637. [gravestone in the Calvinist cemetery in Zychlin near Konin].

PATERSON, DAVID, a trader in Tarnow, in Lvov in 1623. [SCA.100]

PATERSON, JAMES, a doctor of theology, a lecturer at the College of Kedainiai in 1629. [SCA.229]

PATERSON, JAMES, with a house on Konska Street, Kedainiai Market Square, in 1663. [SCA.247]

PATERSON, JOHN, was admitted as a burgess of Poznan, [Posen], in 1589.

PATERSON, THOMAS, master of the Thomas of Dundee, trading between Dundee and Koningsberg [Kaliningrad] in 1684. [NRS.E72.7.11/12]

PATERSON, WALKER, and Company, merchants in Leith, trading with Riga, 1819-1821, sederunt book. [NRS.CS96.897]

PATTON, CHRISTOPHER, was admitted as a member of the Merchant Guild of Konigsberg on 6 January 1659.

PATON, JOHN, master of the Friendship of Pittenweem, trading with Danzig [now Gdansk] in 1749, 1750. [NRS.E504.3.2]

PATRICK, JAMES, master of the James and Margaret of Dundee, trading between Riga and Dundee in 1765, 1766, 1767. [NRS.E504.11.5]

PATULLO, [Betollack], ELISABETH, from Dundee, was married in Gros Nebrau, Danzig, [Gdansk], on 7 October 1640.

PATULLO, GEORGE, in Riga, a letter to Bishop John Falconer at Carnbee, dated 26 October 1722. [NRS.GB254.Br.ms3.dc59/5]

PATULLO, ROBERT, master of the Blackwood of Dundee, trading between Konigsberg [Kaliningrad] and Dundee in 1755; master of the Buxton of Dundee, trading between St Petersburg and Dundee in 1755; master of the Active of Dundee, trading between Riga and Dundee in 1769; master of the Nelly of Dundee trading between Dundee and Riga in 1777. [NRS.E504.11.7/9]

PEARSON, ALEXANDER, a Scot, matriculated at the University of Greifswald in 1622.

PEARSON, DAVID, master of the Margaret of Dundee, trading between Konigsberg [Kaliningrad] and Dundee in 1612, with Danzig [Gdansk] in 1615; master of the Robert of Dundee trading between Danzig and Dundee in 1617. [DSL]

PEARSON, DAVID, died in St Petersburg. [no date] [Anstruther Easter gravestone]

PEARSON, GEORGE, master of the Fortune of Montrose, from Danzig [Gdansk] to Montrose in 1712. [CTB.26.288]

PEARSON, JAMES, a merchant in Riga, son of Robert Pearson of Balmadies, Angus, a sasine, 1768. [NRS.RS35.22.440]

PEDDIE, ANDREW, master of the Virgin of Dundee trading between Danzig [Gdansk] and Dundee in 1772. [NRS.E504.11.8]

PEDDIE, DAVID, a Scot, matriculated at the University of Greifswald in 1546.

PEEBLES, JOHN, master of the Thistle of Irvine, a charter party with Daniel Mussenden, a merchant in Belfast, to transport a cargo of oats or oatmeal to Riga, on 18 April 1734. [PRONI.D354.396]

PENNICUIK, THOMAS, was admitted as a Member of the Merchant Guild of Konigsberg on 28 March 1662.

PERSHAW, DAVID, master of the Gordon of Leith, a privateer operating between Archangel, Bergen, Riga and Cadiz between 1707 and 1712. [MHS.134][NRS.AC10.73; AC9.305][TNA.HCA.26.13]

PETERS, Captain, master of the Mercury bound from Riga with a cargo of grain to Dundee in 1847. [MD.167]

PETRIE, DAVID, master of the Hope, trading between Danzig [Gdansk] and Montrose in 1771, 1772, 1773, [NRS.CE53.1.8]

PETRIE, [Petray], GEORGE, a trader in Tarnow in the 1640s. [SCA.100]

PETRIE, WILLIAM, master of the Robert and Anne of Montrose, trading between Riga and Montrose in 1750. [NRS.E504.24.2]

PHILIP II, Duke of Pomerania, at Bardi, a letter to King James VI of Scotland, dated 11 April 1591. [NRS.GD249.2.3/8]

PIRIE, JOHN, master of the Lyon of Aberdeen trading between Aberdeen and Danzig [Gdansk] in 1691. [NRS.E71.1.20]

PITCAIRN, ROBERT, born 1767, from Perth, a merchant, was admitted as a burger of Klaipedia in 1807. [JSM]

POLLOCK, ..., master of the Happy Chance of Irvine trading between Danzig, [Gdansk], and Irvine in 1752. [AJ.238]

POLMAN, JOHN, in Narva, a letter, 6 February 1726. [PRONI.D654.B2.41]

PORTEOUS, ROBERT, a merchant in Poland, left a legacy to Dalkeith Kirk in 1664. [NRS.GD328.3]; a merchant in Danzig before 1664. [NRS.GD297.116]

PRATT, WILLIAM, master of the Mermaid of Aberdeen trading between Aberdeen and Danzig [Gdansk] in 1690, master of the Janet trading between Danzig and Aberdeen in 1691. [NRS.E72.1.18/19]

PRESTON, JAMES, a skipper, from Montrose to Konigsberg [Kaliningrad] in 1680. [RAK/STR]

PRINGLE, JOHN, [Ian Prengiel], in Pinczow and Mirow, in Cracow in 1619. [SCA.93]

RADDOCH [?], CHRISTOPHER, son of Daniel Radch, a Scot, and his wife Christina, baptised on 15 February 1655 in Tilsit, [Sovetsk]. [Tilsit Reformed Church Records]

RAINY, JAMES, of the Scottish Brotherhood in Konigsberg in 1701. [SIG]

RAIT, JOHN, of the Scottish Brotherhood in Konigsberg in 1701. [SIG]

RALSTON, ROBERT, and ROBERT SMITH, merchants in Ayr, trading with Danzig and Memel, 1789-1807. [NRS.CS96.654-669]

RAMAGE, ANDREW, of the Scottish Brotherhood in Konigsberg in 1701. [SIG]

RAMADGE, THOMAS, of the Scottish Brotherhood in Konigsberg in 1701. [SIG]

RAMEL, HENRICUS, at Wolfenbuttel on 9 April 1591, a letter to Sir John Maitland of Thirlstane. [NRS.GD249.2.3/7]

RAMMECK, [?], WILLIAM, a Scottish lance corporal under Baron von Eiglenburg, married Barbara Miller, widow of Johan Smeling, in the Burgkirche of Koningsberg on 27 June 1667. [Burgkirche Marriage Register]

RAMSAY, ALEXANDER, master of the Thomas and Elizabeth of Dundee, trading between Riga and Dundee in 1737, [NRS.CE70.1.2]; master of the Jean of Dundee, trading between Riga and Dundee in 1743, [NRS.E504.11.1]

RAMSAY, ALEXANDER, master of the Catherine trading between Memel [Klaipeda] and Dundee in 1780. [NRS.E504.11.9]

RAMSAY, CHARLES, of the Scottish Brotherhood in Konigsberg in 1701. [SIG]

RAMSAY, DAVID, master of the David of Dundee, trading with Riga in 1734. [NRS.CE52.1.3/4]

RAMSAY, GILBERT, was admitted as member of the Merchant Guild of Konigsberg on 27 February 1669.

RAMSAY, JAMES, a shopkeeper in Kedainiai, Lithuania, from 1648 until his death in 1664. [SCL.349]

RAMSAY, Captain JAMES, a Scot, married Maria, daughter of Thomas Hall, in St Elizabeth's, Danzig, [Gdansk], on 3 August 1654.

RAMSAY, JOHN, [Jan Ramza], a merchant in Sandomierz around 1600. [SCA.96]

RAMSAY, PATRICK, master of the Elizabeth of Prestonpans, trading between Danzig [Gdansk] and Leith in 1691. [NRS.E72.15.44]

RAMSAY, ROBERT, master of the Friendship of Perth, trading between Perth and Danzig [now Gdansk] in 1724. [NRS.CE52.1.3/4]

RAMSAY, THOMAS, in Kedainiai, 16.. [SCA.236]

RAMSAY, WILLIAM, was buried in St Johann's, Danzig, in 1612.

RAMSAY, WILLIAM, a teacher in Kedainiai, Lithuania, in 1629. [SCL.348]

RAMSAY, WILLIAM, [Wilhelm Ramse], a Scot, married Euphemia ....., in Tragheim, Konigsberg, [Kaliningrad], on 7 February 1638.

RANKEILLOR, JOHN, master of the Three Brothers of Poole, trading between Konigsberg [now Kaliningrad] and Aberdeen in 1752. [NRS.E504.1.4]

RANKINE, ROBERT, master of the Providence of Dundee, trading between Dundee and Konigsberg [Kaliningrad] in 1689. [NRS.E72.7.23]

RANKIN, ROBERT, master of the Joseph of Dundee, bound for Danzig [Gdansk] in 1722, 1723. [NRS.E508]

REDDIE, JOHN, master of the Europa of Dysart, trading between Perth, and Memel [now Klaipeda] in 1767. [NRS.E504.27.5]

RAE, KATHERINA, daughter of John Rae, [Hans Rehe], a Scot, and his wife Mary, was baptised in St Elizabeth's, Danzig, [Gdansk] on 5 September 1632, godparents were Eva

Zander, Katherine Dempster, Christina Balfour, William Balfour, James Lyon, James Mair, and John Scott.

REID, ALEXANDER, from Edinburgh, was admitted as a burgess of Poznan, [Posen], in 1585.

REID, ALEXANDER, a hide trader in Tarnow in 1640s. [SCA.100]

REID, ALEXANDER, master of the Friendship of Cellardyke, trading between Anstruther and Danzig [now Gdansk] in 1750, 1753, 1754, 1756, [NRS.E504.3.2/3], and of the Friendship of Anstruther, trading between Anstruther and Danzig [now Gdansk] in 1749. [NRS.E504.3.2]

REID, ALEXANDER, a merchant in Leith, trading with Danzig, [Gdansk], and joint owner of the Gallert Argo of Stettin [Szczecin] between 1838 and 1839. [NRS.CS96.4287]

REID JOHN, master of the Barbara of Dundee, trading between Dundee and Konigsberg [Kaliningrad] in 1681, 1682. [NRS.E72.7.12]

REID, JOHN, master of the Defiance of Anstruther, trading between Aberdeen and Danzig [now Gdansk] in 1749, 1753, 1759. [NRS.E504.3.2/3/4]

REID, JOHN, master of the Friendship of Peterhead, trading between Aberdeen and Danzig [now Gdansk] in 1748, 1749, 1750. [NRS.E504.1.2/3]

REID, Captain, master of the Hero bound from Riga with a cargo of grain to Dundee in 1847. [MD.167]

REID, Captain, master of the Ratho bound from Riga with a cargo of flax to Dundee in 1847. [MD.167]

REINTROCH, Captain PAUL, master of bark Caroline Fredericke of Danzig, [Gdansk] a petition for a survey, 19 December 1825. [NRS.SC12.6.1825.100]

RENNIE, CHARLES, master of the Providence of Leith, trading between Danzig [Gdansk] and Leith in 1689. [NRS.E72.15.41]

RENNY, JOHN, master of the Jean and Peggy, trading between Riga and Montrose in 1771, 1773. [NRS.CE53.5/8]

RICHARDSON, [Ritscheschon], CATHERINE, married R. Dickson, in St Elisabeth's, Danzig, [Gdansk], on 28 November 1639.

RIDDELL, FRANCIS, in a letter to Hugh Scott, mentions a possible claim to an estate in Livonia, on the Gulf of Riga, on 14 December 1815. [NRS.GD157.2347]

RITCHIE, ANDREW, master of the Two Brothers of Fraserburgh, trading between Aberdeen and Danzig [now Gdansk] in 1750. [NRS.E504.1.3]

RITCHIE, ANNA, daughter of Hans Ritsch, a Scot, [John Ritchie], was baptised in Tilsit [Sovetsk] on 28 November 1668, godfathers were James Somer, William and Albert Ritchie, and Alexander Crichton. [Tilsit Reformed Church Records]

RITCHIE, JAMES, of the Scottish Brotherhood in Konigsberg in 1701. [SIG]

RITCHIE, JAMES, [Jacob Ritsch], a Scot, died of the plague in Elbing, [Elblag], in September 1710.

RITCHIE, JOHN, master of the Farmer of Arbroath, trading between Danzig [Gdansk] and Montrose in 1750. [NRS.E504.24.2]

ROBERTSON, ANDREW, [Andr. Rupertsen], a Scot, was father of Andrew who was baptised in the Lutheran Church in Insterburg on 22 September 1621.

ROBERTSON, ANDREW, master of the Amity, trading between Memel [Klaipeda] and Dundee in 1783. [NRS.E504.11.11]

ROBERTSON, GEORGE, master of the Moncreiff of Leith, trading between Riga and Dundee in 1766. [NRS.E504.11.3]

ROBERTSON, GILBERT, a merchant in Edinburgh, trading with Danzig and the Baltic lands between 1690 and 1694. [NRS.CS96.1726]

ROBERTSON, JACOB, a journeyman merchant in Danzig, [Gdansk], died there on 27 March 1658. [Gdansk Archives, 300, R/Vv 191.28-36]

ROBERTSON, JAMES, master of the Sophia of Anstruther, trading between Anstruther and Danzig [now Gdansk] in 1744. [NRS.E504.3.1]

ROBERTSON, JOHN, [Hans Robbartsen] a Scot, married Catherine, daughter of Waltin Hein, in Altstadt, Konigsberg, [Kaliningrad] on 27 November 1605.

ROBERTSON, JOHN, married Margaret, a servant, daughter of ..... Horne in Aberdeen, in St Elisabeth's, Danzig, [Gdansk], on 27 August 1641.

ROBERTSON, JOHN, married Anna, daughter of Hans Mieler, in Heilig Leichnam, Danzig, [Gdansk], in 1645.

ROBERTSON, JOHN, master of the Red Lion of Queensferry, trading between Danzig [Gdansk] and Leith in 1691. [NRS.E72.15.44]

ROBERTSON, WILLIAM, master of the Buxton of Dundee, trading between Stettin [now Szczecin] and Dundee in 1766. [NRS.E504.11.6]

ROBERTSON, THOMAS, a Scot, married Elisabeth daughter of Hans Boggensen, in Tragheim, Konigsberg, [Kaliningrad], on 1 September 1653.

ROBERTSON, WILLIAM, in Kedainiai, Lithuania, between 1649 and 1659. [SCL.356]

'RODT' [?], THOMAS, a Scots pedlar, married Elisabeth, daughter of Andreas Keusse, in Altstadt, Konigsberg, [Kaliningrad], in December 1611.

ROGERS, JAMES, a physician in St Petersburg, son and heir of James Rogers, a wright in Hamilton, Lanarkshire, who died in August 1851, also grand nephew of Thomas Rogers a merchant in Edinburgh. [NRS.S/H]

ROGERSON, ALEXANDER, in St Petersburg, letters, 1817, 1824, 1827. [NRS.GD1.620.9/31/130]

ROGERSON, Dr, in St Petersburg, a letter, 1802. [NRS.GD1.620.2]

ROLLO, JOHN, master of the <u>Humphrey of Dundee,</u> trading between Riga and Dundee in 1748. [NRS.E504.11.1]

ROLLO, ROBERT, master of the <u>Humphrey of Dundee,</u> trading between Riga and Dundee in 1746. [NRS.E504.11.1]

ROMANOV, MICHAEL, Archduke of Russia, was admitted as a burgess and guilds-brother of Ayr on 25 February 1818. [ABR]

RONALD, JAMES, [Jacob Rhonald], a trader in Tarnow, in Lvov in 1627. [SCA.100]

ROSS, ALEXANDER, a trader in Opatow, at the Rzeszow fair in 1650. [SAP.99][SCA.92]

ROSS, ALEXANDER, a merchant in Cracow, husband of Sophia French, parents of Alexander and David, returned to Scotland and settled at Easter Kindeace in Easter Ross, in 1721. [SAP.96]

ROSS, ANDREW, a burgher of Tarnow in 1599, in Cracow from 1599 to 1603. [SCA.100]

ROSS, ANDREW, master of the Elspet of Dundee trading between Danzig [Gdansk] and Dundee in1618. [DSL]

ROSS, CHRISTIAN, a merchant and citizen of Varso, [Warsaw], in 1699. [SAP.98].

ROSS, DANIEL, son of Daniel Ross a Scotsman, was baptised in the Reformed Church in Tilsit [Sovetsk] on 14 December 1651.

ROSS, GEORGE, an elder of the Scots Presbyterian Brotherhood in Lublin in 1701-1726. [SAP.99]

ROSS, GEORGE, a member of the Merchants Guild of Konigsberg [Kaliningrad] in 1723. [SAP.98]

ROSS, HENRY, a merchant in Tarnow during the 1620s. [SCA.100]

ROSS, JACOB, a merchant in Tarnow in 1620s. [SCA.100]

ROSS, JOHN, in Chmielnik in 1651. [SCA.89]

ROSS, MARGARET, wife of Admiral Thomas Gordon of the Russian Navy, died before 8 January 1722. [NRS.GD24.1.859]

ROSS, ROBERT, in Vilnius, Lithuania, from 1646 to 1652. [SCL.357]

ROSS, ROBERT, master of the Buxton of Dundee, trading between Riga and Montrose in1748. [NRS.E504.24.2]

ROSS, THOMAS, master of the Blessing, trading between Konigsberg [Kaliningrad] and Dundee in 1643. [DSL]

ROSS, THOMAS, a merchant in Montrose trading with Riga, sederunt book, 1819-1820. [NRS.CS96.819]

ROSS, WILLIAM, master of the Blessing, trading between Konigsberg [Kaliningrad] and Dundee in 1643. [DSL]

ROSS, WILLIAM, postmaster of Cracow in 1707, was probably killed at nearby Myslenice in 1707. [SAP.99]

ROSS, WILLIAM, master of the Bon Accord of Aberdeen, trading between Danzig [now Gdansk] and Aberdeen in 1742. [NRS.E504.1.1]

ROSS, WILLIAM, from Ireland but in Poland, was reported 'to be in good health', in a letter dated 8 November 1661. [NRS.GD406.1.9695]

ROSS, WILLIAM, an alderman of Kedainai, Lithuania, co-founder of a trading company for Protestants in 1731. [SAP.98]

RULE, JAMES, [Jac. Roule], 'Schotsekret'. Married Justina Foster, a widow, in St Marien Kirche, Elbing, [Elblag], on 1 May 1689.

RUSSELL, ALEXANDER, from Aberdeen, matriculated at the University of Greifswald in 1519.

RUSSELL, ANDREW, MD, settled in a suburb of Radom in 1608, he was dead before 24 March 1626 when his daughter Elisabeth was christened, father of Paul baptized on 30 June 1622, and Kristin. [SCA.94]

RUSSELL, GEORGE, master of the Lyon of Pittenweem, was employed by Ernst Melsuo, a merchant in Riga, to transport a cargo from there to St Malo in October 1680, which was never delivered, a case before the High Court of the Admiralty of Scotland on 18 October 1686. [NRS.AC7.8]

RUSSELL, DANIEL, in Szydlowiec, from 1614 to 1647, married Agnieszka Abrachamowska in 1640. [SCA.97]

RUSSELL, JACOB, son of Alexander Russel a burgher of Sydlowiec, a merchant and sub bailiff at Opoczno, he was in Radom in 1631, died in 1647. [SCA.92]

RUSSELL, JOHN, a servant in Radom around 1648 to 1651. [SCA.94]

RUSSELL, Captain, a soldier in Memel in February 1631. [JSM]

RUTHERFORD, GEORGE, master of the Christian of Dysart, trading between Danzig [Gdansk] and Dundee in 1765. [NRS.E504.11.6]; master of the George of Dysart, trading between Perth and Viborg, Russia, in 1766, 1767. [NRS.E504.27.5]

RUTHERFORD, THOMAS, [Thomas Ritterpfordt], a malt brewer from Scotland, in Angerburg in 1659.

RUTHVEN, [Riven], ELIZABETH, daughter of John Ruthven [Hans Riven] and his wife Catherine, was baptised in St Elizabeth's, Danzig, [Gdansk] on 11 December 1629.

RUTHVEN, Colonel FRANK, [Franz Ruthuen], Military Governor of Memel in 1629. [JSM]

RUTHVEN, GEORGE, [Georg Rawen], a broad cloth weaver journeyman from Scotland, married Racel Bedau the widow of Joachim Lewen a soldier, in Tragheim, Konigsberg, [Kaliningrad] on 24 November 1641.

RUTHVEN, Colonel JOHN, subscribed to a bond of 12,000 rix dollars, in favour of his wife Barbara Leslie, witnessed by Lieutenant James King, Major Alexander Leslie, and Archibald Colville, in Stettin, [Szczecin], Prussia, on 6 May 1631. [NRS.GD26.4.41]

RUTHVEN, Sir PATRICK, [Pater Rotwein], born 1586, a soldier in the service of Sweden from 1606, fought in Livonia and Russia, Swedish Quartermaster General in 1615. Colonel of the

Kalmar Regiment in 1623, was knighted on the battlefield by Gustavus Adolphus, Commander of a Scottish Regiment in Elbing [Elblag] and Memel [Klaipeda] from 1629 to 1630, a letter from Memel to Lord Ogilvy dated 1614; a Lieutenant General in the service of Gustavus Adolphus in the 1630s, defeated the Saxons at Domitz in 1635, returned to Britain during 1636, a General under King Charles I, was appointed Earl of Forth and Brentford, died in Dundee on 2 February 1651. [Monifieth gravestone][SIS.40] [NRS.GD16.34.12]

SAMSON, DAVID, in Ilza in 1639. [SCA.90]

SAMSON, RICHARD, a servant of David Walwood, in Kunow in 1651. [SCA.92]

SANDER, JOHN, a Scot, married Elisabeth the widow of James Kittrick, on 12 April 1627 in St Elizabeth's, Danzig, [Gdansk].

SANGSTER, ANDREW, a burgher of Skrzynno in 1642. [SCA.97]

SANGSTER, MARGARET, wife of Alexander Russell a councillor of Szydlowiec, died in 1620. [SCA.97]

SAUNDERS and MELLIS, merchants in Aberdeen, trading with St Petersburg, Archangel, and Riga, around 1826. [NRS.CS96.417.15]; sederunt book, 1819-1829. [NRS.CS96.417.1-21]

SCONE, EDWARD, [Eduardus Schonerus], from Edinburgh, matriculated at the University of Greifswald in 1623.

SCONE, JOHN, [Johannes Schonerus], from Edinburgh, matriculated at the University of Greifswald in 1635.

SCOTT, ALEXANDER, a shipmaster trading between Dundee and Riga in 1576, and with Konigsberg [Kaliningrad] in 1578; trading between Nieuwpoort in Flanders and Riga in 1576, and

between Bruges, Flanders, and Danzig [Gdansk] in 1578.
[RAK/STR]

SCOTT, ALEXANDER, trading between Dundee and Konigsberg, Danzig, and Riga, 1577, 1578, [RAK/STR]; master of the Benjamin of Montrose, trading between Konigsberg [Kaliningrad] and Montrose in 1683, 1684. [NRS.E72.16.12]

SCOTT, DAVID, in Vilnius, Lithuania, in 1631. [SCL.359]

SCOTT, DAVID, master of the Alison of Dundee, trading between Anstruther and Danzig [now Gdansk] in 1745. [NRS.E504.3.1]

SCOTT, HARRIET, of Harden, Berwickshire, received a letter from Prince Adam Czartoryski, then in London, dated 26 February 1833. [NRS.GD157.2455]

SCOTT, JAMES, married Elisabeth, daughter of Lucas Sinnogh, of Pythau, in St Elisabeth's, Danzig, [Gdansk], on 9 May 1639.

SCOTT, JAMES, the British minister in Poland, dispatches, 1715. [NRS.NRAS.2171.14553]; a letter to Stanhope dated October 1720. [NRS.GD158.1902]

SCOTT, JOHN, [Hans Schott], a burgess of Newenburg, married Maria, daughter of Hans Eckwald in Marienburg, in St Elisabeth's, Danzig, [Gdansk], on 17 October 1640.

SCOTT, JOHN, [Hans Schott], son of Hans Schott and his wife Regina, was baptised in the Reformed Church of SS Peter and Paul in Danzig [Gdansk] on 11 November 1650, godparent was Margaret, a Scot from Konigsberg, [Kaliningrad].

SCOTT, JOHN, a barber in Cracow in 1677-1679, was granted honorary citizenship of Cracow. [SAP.103]

SCOTT, JOHN, of Scalloway, Shetland, agent for Captain Michael Teolcke late of the <u>Columbus of Danzig,</u> a petition dated 3 April 1800. [Shetland Archives.SC12.6.1800.41]

SCOTT, MICHAEL, married Dorothea, widow of George Thiun, in Danzig in 1666. [Aller Gottes Engel records]

SCOTT, PATRICK, master of the <u>Elizabeth of Dundee,</u> trading between Riga and Dundee in 1750. [NRS.E504.11.2]

SCOTT, PETER, married Anna Grau, in St Bartholemew's, Danzig, [Gdansk], on 28 April 1577.

SCOTT, ROBERT, a manufacturer nd flax spinner in Cupar, Fife, trading with Archangel between 1826 and 1837. [NRS.CS96.785]

SCOTT, STEPHEN, born in Norfolk, Virginia, a Captain of the Russian Navy, died in Kronstadt, Russia, in 1818. [S.83.18]

SCRYMGEOUR, [Scringer], JOHN, a poor man in Ilza in 1651. [SCA.90]

SCRYMGEOUR, JOHN, [Jan Krumzer], with a house on Konska Street, Kedainiai Market Square, in 1663. [SCA.147]

SCRYMGEOUR, THOMAS, born 1616 in Errol, Perthshire, a merchant in Kedainiai, Lithuania, from 1649 to 1668. [SCL.360]; with a house on Konska Street, Kedainiai Market Square in 1663. [SCA.247]

SETON, ERASMUS, [Erasmus Sethon], a trader in Cracow from 1602 until 1605, a citizen of Tarnow in1605. [SCA.100]

SETON, WILLIAM, in Kedainiai, Lithuania, in 1679. [SCL.362]

SHAIRP, JAMES, in Danzig, [Gdansk], a letter, dated 12 July 1679.to his father William Shairp of Houston. [NRS.GD30.1543]

SHAIRP, WALTER, a merchant in St Petersburg, son of Thomas Shairp of Houston, letters, between 1744 and 1771. [NRS.GD30.1583]

SHARP, JOHN, a merchant in Kedainiai, Lithuania, from 1668 to 1706. [SCL.362]

SHAW, DAVID, a shipmaster trading between Montrose and Konigsberg [Kaliningrad] in 1620, 1627, and 1628. [RAK/STR]

SHEARER, PATRICK, son of William Shearer and his wife Janet Brown in Auchenleck, Kinnoir, a resident of Elbing, Prussia, in 1599. [MSC.II.48]

SHEPARD, JAMES, a Scottish shipmaster trading between Flanders and Konigsberg [Kaliningrad] in 1577. [RAK/STR]

SHEPHERD, GEORGE, master of the Christian of Perth, trading between Perth and Memel [now Klaipeda], and with Danzig [now Gdansk] in 1758, 1760; master of the Eagle of Perth, trading between Perth and Danzig [now Gdansk] in 1763. [NRS.E504.27.3/4]

SCHETKY, GEORGE, born in Edinburgh in June 1776, son of J. G. S. Schetky and his wife Maria Reinagle, married Elizabeth Paterson, daughter of Stephen Paterson, in Philadelphia in 1823. [SM.91.518]

SHEWAN, DAVID, master of the Greenboom of Montrose, trading between Konigsberg [Kaliningrad] and Montrose in 1669. [NRS.E72.16.3]

SHORT, HENRY, master of the Alison of Dundee, trading between Anstruther and Danzig [now Gdansk] in 1744. [NRS.E504.3.1]

SIBBALD, JAMES, [Jacob Szybalt], in Szydlowiec was married to Ann Russell, from 1639 to 1651. [SCA.98]

SIME, JAMES, master of the Aurora of Dundee, when bound from Riga to Lisbon in 1798 was captured by a French privateer. [AJ.665]

SIMSON, ANDREW, a merchant in Kedainiai, Lithuania, from 1636 until his death in 1656. [SCL.363]

SIMPSON, ANDREW, formerly a shipmaster in Leith, then Commander of the Navy of the Czar of Russia, a deed, 1706. [NRS.RD3.69.311]

SIMSON, DAVID, a merchant in Kedainiai, Lithuania, from 1637 until 1653. [SCL.364]

SIMPSON, DAVID, master of the Jean of Dundee, trading between Riga and Dundee in 1764, trading between Swinnemund in Pomerania and Dundee in 1765. [NRS.E504.11.5]

SIMSON, JAMES, married Anna, daughter of Simon Fentzke, in St Marien Kirche, Danzig, [Gdansk], on 12 May 1651.

SIMPSON, JAMES, master of the Albany of Leith, from Leith to Danzig, [Gdansk], in 1681. [PL]

SIMSON, JOHN, master of the Humility of Greenock, from Greenock to Danzig [now Gdansk] in 1741. [CM.3377]

SIMPSON, JOHN and HENRY, merchants in Memel, a letter, 1769, trading with James Morrison and Company in Perth. [NRS.B59.37.9.4]

SIMPSON, JOSEPH, master of the Happy Isabel of Fraserburgh, trading between Aberdeen and Danzig [now Gdansk] in 1750. [NRS.E504.1.3]

SIMPSON, LUDWIG, in Memel, [Klaipeda], a client of D. and J.H. Campbell, solicitors in Edinburgh, between 1800 and 1806. [NRS.GD253.212]

SIMPSON, WILLIAM, [Wilhelm Simmson], a Scottish soldier, married Elisabeth, daughter of Wilhelm Moritz, in St Elizabeth's, Danzig, [Gdansk] on 22 May 1633.

SIMPSON, MCLEAN, and Company, merchants in Memel, 1790. [NRS.B59.37.9.24]

SIMPSON, Captain, master of the brig Victoria was lost at sea on 14 September 1843 when bound from Dundee to Memel. [MD.157]

SIMPSON, Captain, master of the Jessie bound from Riga with a cargo of grain to Dundee in 1847. [MD.167]

SINCLAIR, ALBERT, a merchant in Sandomierz in 1587. [SCA.96]

SINCLAIR, DAVID, to Sweden in 1651, a cavalry officer who was killed at the Battle of Warsaw in 1656. [SHR.ix.275]

SINCLAIR, HENRY, a Scot, matriculated at the University of Konigsberg [Kaliningrad] in 1619.

SINCLAIR, Lord HENRY, and James Oswald, the Provost of Kirkcaldy, with a cargo of salt, with a bill of lading, bound for Danzig [Gdansk] on 20 February 1706. [NRS.GD164.515]; later, on 14 October 1706, they entered a charter party with Henry Oswald the younger, master of the Isabel of Kirkcaldy for a voyage to Danzig, [Gdansk]. [NRS.GD164.415]

SINCLAIR, ROBERT, of the 93rd [Sutherland Highlanders] Regiment, a notebook of 1854 concerning the Crimean War. [NRS.RH4.141]

SINCLAIR, Captain, master of the brig British King of Dundee when bound from Dundee to Riga became stranded at Noen near Arildsloga on 30 April 1844. [MD.160]

SKENE, CATHERINE, daughter of the late David Skene, a merchant in Zamoski, Poland, brother of George Skene of Wester Fintray, and David Aedie late Treasurer of Aberdeen, a marriage contract, dated 27 March 1674. [NRS.GD244.1.64]

SKENE, DAVID, a Scot, was admitted as a burgess of Poznan, [Posen], in 1586.

SKENE, Sir GEORGE, of Fintray, subscribed to a Bond of Provision, on 8 November 1697, in favour of Alexander Skene, son of the late David Skene a merchant in Poland, his brother, of 4000 merks secured over the lands of Wester Fintray, under a marriage contract of 8 February 1690. [NRS.GD244.1.261]

SKENE, Sir JOHN, a letter from Munius Eusebius stating that he went into exile in West Pomerania and later in Prentzlau, letter dated 20 February 1595 in Prenzlau. [NRS.RH9.2.179]

SKLAITT, ANDREW, son of Robert Sklaitt and his wife Katherine Steven in Udny, Ellon, Aberdeenshire, died in Brynnusser, Premissill, Poland, in 1599. [MSC.II.46]

SMALL, HENRY, an engineer from Dundee, in St Petersburg, Russia, a sasine, 20 September 1875. [NRS.RS.Auchtermuchty.6.228]

SMITH, ALEXANDER, [Alexander Schmidt], a Scot, married Anna, daughter of Gregor Darkau, in Altstadt, Konigsberg, [Kaliningrad], on 31 January 1608.

SMITH, ANDREW, born in Scotland, a journeyman merchant, married Maria, the widow of Mathis Valentine, were married in Danzig, [Gdansk], on 21 February 1678. [Aller Gottes Engel records]

SMITH, A., of the Scottish Brotherhood in Konigsberg in 1701. [SIG]

SMITH, DAVID, master of the Elizabeth of Montrose, trading between Danzig [Gdansk] and Montrose, in 1682. [NRS.E72.16.10]

SMITH, GEORGE, in Kedainiai, Lithuania, in 1637. [SCL.365]

SMITH, JAMES, master of the Charming Lily of Dundee, trading between Dundee and Riga in 1753, with Narva in 1753; master of the Merry Plowman of Dundee from Dundee to Danzig [Gdansk] in 1755. [NRS.E504.11]

SMITH, JOHN, master of the Jean of Pittenweem, trading between Anstruther and Riga in 1759, 1761, 1762, and with Danzig [now Gdansk] in 1761. [NRS.E504.3.3]

SMITH, JOHN, born in 1800, died in Moscow on 17 February 1878. [Greenock gravestone]

SMITH, PETER, a merchant trafficker in Prussia, in August 1629. [NRS.AC7.2.223]

SMITH, PETER, master of the Frau Van Kalcreuth Von Memel, from Greenock to St Thomas in the Danish West Indies in November 1782. [NRS.E504.15.37]

SMITH, RICHARD, master of the Richard and Anne trading between Memel [Klaipeda] and Dundee in 1783. [NRS.E504.11.10], daughter of Niclas Biston on 24 April 1651 in St Elizabeth's, Danzig, [Gdansk].

SMITH, Captain, master of the Mary bound from Riga with a cargo of flax to Dundee in 1847. [MD.167]

SMYTH, PATRICK, son of Patrick Smyth of Braco, Orkney, a servant of Alexander Johnston a cloth merchant in Danzig in 1647. [NRS.GD190.2.186]

SMYTOUN, JOSEPH, master of the Post of Dundee, trading between Dundee and Konigsberg [Kaliningrad] in 1683, and the Katherine of Dundee, trading between Konigsberg [Kaliningrad] and Dundee in 1684. [NRS.E72.7.17]

SOMERVILLE, JAMES, a merchant in Kedainiai, Lithuania, from late 1640s util his death in 1684. [SCL.365]

SOUTAR, ..., master of the Lovely Katie of Peterhead from Peterhead to Danzig [Gdansk] in 1783. [AJ.1853]

SPEED, LACHLAN, a Scot, in Mohrungen, was godparent to Louisa, daughter of George Lessel and his wife Maria Douglas, in Soldau on 22 November 1729.

SPENS, JAMES, son of James Spens in Edinburgh, a drum major in Swedish service in Doesburg, Riga, Amsterdam and Batavia, from 1617 to 1632. [NRS.RH9.2,231-4]

SPINK, ANDREW, master of the Nelly of Dundee, trading between St Petersburg and Dundee in 1770, trading between Riga and Dundee in 1773, 1774, 1775, 1776, 1777. [NRS.E504.11.8/9/10]

SPINK, JOHN, son of John Spink, a Scot, and his wife Gertrud, was baptised in St Elizabeth's, Danzig, [Gdansk] on 16 September 1629.

SPINK, JAMES, master of the Cecilia of Arbroath, trading between Konigsberg [Kaliningrad] and Montrose in 1744, [NRS.E504.24.11]

SPINK, JOHN, master of the Fortune of Arbroath, trading between Riga and Montrose in 1742; master of the Cecilia of Arbroath, trading between Konigsberg [Kaliningrad] and Montrose in 1744 [NRS.E504.24.1]; master of the Betty and Susan, trading between Riga and Montrose in1771, 1772. [NRS.CE53.1.5/8]

SPITTAL, ANDREW, master of the Peggy of Dysart trading between Memel [Klaipeda] and Dundee in 1776. [NRS.E504.11.9]

SPITTAL, ROBERT, master of the Diligence of Kincardine-on-Forth, trading with St Petersburg, Archangel, Vyborg, and Danzig, [Gdansk], 1805-1807. Logbook. [NRS.CS96.3345]

STEPHEN, JAMES, master of the Mansfield of Crail, trading between Anstruther and Memel [now Klaipeda] in 1766, with Danzig [now Gdansk] in 1767, with Konigsberg [now Kaliningrad] in 1769. [NRS.E504.3.3/4]

STEUART, JOHN, a merchant and baillie of Inverness, trading with Danzig in 1720s. [see 'The Letterbook of Baillie John Steuart, 1715-1752', Edinburgh, 1915]

STEVENSON, PATRICK, master of the St Peter, trading between Konigsberg [Kaliningrad] and Dundee in 1642. [DSL]

STEWART, ALEXANDER, master of the Dundee, trading between Riga and Dundee in 1737. [NRS.CE70.1.2]

STEWART, ALEXANDER, master of the Charles of Fraserburgh, trading between Aberdeen and Danzig [now Gdansk] in 1747; master of the Pretty Peggy of Fraserburgh, trading from Danzig [now Gdansk] and Aberdeen in 1751, 1752. [NRS.E504.1.2/4]

STEWART, ALEXANDER, master of the John and Mally of Kincardine, trading between Perth and Memel [now Klaipeda] in 1767. [NRS.E504.27.5]

STEWART, JAMES V., King of Scotland wrote to George and Barnim, Dukes of Stettin and Pomerania regarding a captured ship, on 20 June 1533, [NRS.GD149.264.10]; and on 24 May 1542 he wrote to the Magistrates of Anklam [Tanglin] in Pomerania concerning a ship seized by the Scots. [NRS.GD149.264.174]

STEWART, JAMES, letters from Sevastopol, dated 1854-1855. [NRS.GD424.8.17/18/28/37]

STEWART, JOHN, master of the Spier of Greenock, bound from Greenock to Danzig [Gdansk] in 1741. [CM.3374]

STIRLING, ALBERT, [Arbrecht Sterling], a Scot, married Gertrud, widow of … Jochimsen, banns 14 March 1631, Gross Nebrau, Elbing, [Elblag].

STIRLING, GEORGE, a shipmaster trading between Dundee and Konigsberg [Kaliningrad] in 1577, and with Danzig [Gdansk] in 1582. [RAK/STR]

STIRLING, GEORGE, and his brother THOMAS STIRLING, in Tarnow, trading in Wroclaw, [Breslau], and Ruthenia from late 1630s until 1650s. [SCA.101]

STIRLING, Sir HENRY, in St Petersburg, a letter to John Drummond of Quarrel, a Director of the East India Company, in 1729. [NRS.GD24.1.464L]

STIRLING, JOHN, born 1836, son of John Stirling of Eldershaw and his wife Elizabeth Willing, died at Inkerman on 5 November 1854. [St Andrews gravestone]

STIRLING, WILLIAM, a secretary in Oberland, married Anna Catherina, daughter of Johannes Schieneman pastor in Mohrungen, there in 1676.

STOCKDALE, SIMON, master of the Brilliant of Scarborough, trading between Narva and Dundee in 1767. [NRS.E504.11.6]

STRACHAN, BARBARA, was buried in Danzig in 1658. [Aller Gottes Engel records]

STRACHAN, DAVID, a goldsmith in Cracow in 1631. [SAP.81]

STRACHAN, JAMES, a shipmaster trading between Dundee and Konigsberg [Kaliningrad] also Stralsund, and Danzig in 1574. [RAK/STR]

STRACHAN, JAMES, master of the Charming Nelly of Montrose, trading between Riga and Aberdeen in 1751, 1752, [NRS.E504.1.4]

STRACHAN, JOHN, from Aberdeen, married Agnes, daughter of the late John Forbes in Aberdeen, in Heiliger Geist, Danzig, [Gdansk], in 1634.

STRACHAN, JOHN, married Maria, widow of Peter Ulrich, in Heilig Leichnam, Danzig, [Gdansk], in 1640.

STRACHAN, JOHN, in Montrose, formerly in Narva, 1775, son of Lieutenant James Strachan of the Royal Navy, a sasine. [NRS.RS35.25.289]

STRACHAN, THOMAS, married Margaret Kober, in the Burgkirche, Konigsberg, [Kaliningrad], on 16 February 1642.

STRACHAN, THOMAS, from Aberdeen, [Eberthon], and Johanna Bamert, daughter of Peter Bomert a cobbler, were married in Tragheim, Konigsberg, [Kaliningrad], on 17 October 1650. Thomas Strachan a Scot in Mittel Tragheim, was a godfather in Tragheim on 14 February 1652, also there on 21 February 1655.

STRACHAN, TOCKOL, son of Edward Strachan, was buried in Danzig, [Gdansk], in 1655. [Aller Gottes Engel records]

STRATON, JOHN, master of the brig Janet of Montrose, trading between Riga and Montrose in 1773. [NRS.CE53.1.8]

STRONOCH, ROBERT, of the Scottish Brotherhood in Konigsberg in 1701. [SIG]

STUART, ALEXANDER, a Scot, was granted a passport by King Vladislaus of Poland on 25 October 1634. [NRS.GD103.2.142]

STUART, JAMES, a dealer, married Anna Friese, daughter of Hans Friese 'a Fresian in Samland', in the Burgkirche, Konigsberg, [Kaliningrad], on 26 September 1646.

STUART, Lieutenant, a soldier in Memel in February 1631. [JSM]

SUTTER, PETER, a bond of caution with the owners of the Anne of Archangel in 1812. [NRS.AC11.2295/2321]

SWAN, DAVID, a shipmaster, trading between Montrose and Koningsberg [Kaliningrad] in 1680. [RAK.STR]

SYMMERS, JOHN, master of the Two Brothers of Dundee, trading between Danzig [Gdansk] and Dundee in 1749. [NRS.E504.11.2][CL.367]

TARN, JAMES, of the Scottish Brotherhood in Konigsberg in 1701. [SIG]

TAYLOR, ALEXANDER, in Vilnius, Lithuania, in 1631. [SCL.367]

TAYLOR, [nee Forbes], ELISABETH, died 1723. [gravestone in the Calvinist cemetery in Zychlin near Konin]

TAYLOR, JOHN, a Scottish pedlar in Littau, married Elisabeth Gree, in the Burgkirche, Konigsberg, [Kaliningrad], on 14 July 1647.

TAYLOR, JOHN, an elder at Wielkanoc in 1704. [SAP.81]

TAYLOR, JOHN, died 1716. [gravestone in the Calvinist cemetery in Zychlin near Konin]

TAYLOR, ROBERT, master of the Industry of Anstruther, trading between Anstruther and Danzig [now Gdansk] in 1757, 1761. [NRS.E504.3.3]

TEMPLETON, JOHN, [Hanus Tempelton], a burgher of Szydlowiec in 1607. [SCA.98]

TEVENDALE, ROBERT, was buried in St Peter and Paul's Reformed Church in Danzig in 1686.

TEVENDALE, WILLIAM, was admitted to the Merchant Guild of Konigsberg on 6 July 1700, also, was of the Scottish Brotherhood in Konigsberg in 1701. [SIG]

THOM, ..., master of the Trial of Aberdeen trading between Danzig [Gdansk] and Aberdeen in 1755. [AJ.403]

THOMSON, ALEXANDER, was buried in St Peter and Paul's Reformed Church in Danzig in 1689.

THOMSON, ALEXANDER, master of the Vernon of Aberdeen, trading between Danzig [Gdansk] and Aberdeen in 1742, 1743. [NRS.E504.1.1]

THOMPSON, ANDREW, a merchant in Opatow in 1715. [SCA.92]

THOMSON, ANDREW, master of the Mary trading between St Petersburg and Dundee in 1771. [NRS.E504.11.7]

THOMSON, DAVID, in Kelme, Lithuania, in 1624. [SCL.368]

THOMSON, DAVID, a sailor from Leith, married Elisabeth, daughter of Walter Petersen, on 11 October 1649 in St Elizabeth's, Danzig, [Gdansk].

THOMSON, DAVID, chief engineer on ships of the Russian Post Office, in Viborg, Finland, mainly on the mail steamship 'Vladimir' from 1862 to 1872, papers from 1841, his artwork includes 'The Sugar Mill at Viborg' around 1850. [NRS.GD1.980.2]

THOMSON, ISABELLA, letters from Riga and St Petersburg in 1886. [NRS.GD1.980]

THOMSON, JOHN, a trader in Tarnow in 1632. [SCA.101]

THOMSEN, MICHAEL, in St Petersburg, a letter in Dutch, dated 6 February 1726. [PRONI.D654.B2.41]

THOMSON, PETER, master of the Lyon, trading between Konigsberg, [Kaliningrad], and Dundee in 1639. [DSL]

THOMSON, RICHARD, [Ricardus Tonson], a Scottish merchant, was admitted as a burgess of Poznan, [Posen] in 1597.

THOMSON, THOMAS, master of the Adventure trading between Memel [Klaipeda] and Dundee in 1783. [NRS.E540.11.10]

THORNTON, WILLIAM, master of the Queensberry of Dundee, trading between Riga and Dundee in 1764; master of the Fame of Dundee, from Dundee to the Carolinas in 1773/1777; trading between Riga and Dundee in 1766; master of the Nelly trading between Danzig [Gdansk] and Dundee in 1783. [NRS.E504.11.5/10; CE70.1.6]

TIEDEMAN, CARSTEN, master of the Duke Ernst Johann Von Libau, [now Liepaja] trading between Libau and Perth in 1764, 1765. [NRS.E504.27.5]

TOD, JAMES and ANDREW, grain merchants in Bo'ness, trading with Prussia, financial records, 1809-1817. [NRS.CS96.106-118]; trading with Russia in 1813 to 1816. [NRS.CS96.110]

TOELCKE, Captain MICHAEL, of the Columbus of Danzig a petition in Scalloway, Shetland, on 3 April 1800. [NRS.SC12.6.1800.41]

TORRIE, [Theory], RICHARD, in Pinczow, trading in Ruthenia in 1631. [SCA.94]

TORRIE, WILLIAM, [Wilhelm Thore], a merchant and citizen of Cracow in 1626, married Susanne Orem, born 1612, in Lucianowice in 1629, parents of six children, members of the Reformed Church in Cracow, paid their tithe to King Charles II in 1651. [SAP.71/73/74]

TOURS, JOHAN, Baron von Innerlicht, an old Scottish family, Chamberlain and General, married Barbara, daughter of the late Anthon Schmied, late member of the English company, in St Marien Kirche, Elbing, [Elblag] on 24 February 1671.

TRAILL, JOHN, master of the Lilly of Montrose, trading from Riga to Dundee in 1749. [NRS.E504.11.2]

TRET [?], REGINA, daughter of John Tret from Aberdeen, married Alexander Ross, a soldier, in St Elizabeth's, Danzig, [Gdansk], on 8 November 1646.

TROTTER, J., of the Scottish Brotherhood in Konigsberg in 1701. [SIG]

TURCAN, JAMES, born 1822, son of William Turcan and his wife Catherine Watt, died in Danzig, [Gdansk], on 23 March 1875. [Tulliallan gravestone]

TURNBULL, JOHN, master of the Happy Return of Montrose, bound for Danzig [Gdansk], in 1714, 1715. [NRS.E508]

TURPIE, Captain, master of the Diana bound from Riga with a cargo of grain to Dundee in 1847. [MD.167]

ULRIC, Duke of Mechlenburg, wrote a letter on 8 April 1591 at the Castle of Eustow, to King James VI of Scotland. [NRS.GD249.2.3]

VERSON, family in Estonia, a genealogical memorial sent to Sir John Erskine of Alva in 1725. [NRS.GD80.967]

WALKER, CORNELIUS, a Scottish pedlar, married Barbara, widow of Casper Petsch, in Altstadt, Konigsberg, [Kaliningrad], on 12 October 1603.

WALLACE, DAVID, master of the Hopewell of Arbroath, trading between Riga and Montrose in 1750. [NRS.E504.24.2]

WALLACE, PETER, [Piotr Walls], in Cracow, paid their tithe to King Charles II in 1651. [SAP.71]

WALLACE, Captain, master of the Blossom bound from Riga with a cargo of flax to Dundee in 1847. [MD.167]

WALWOOD, ADAM, a servant of Bartholomew Wood in Tarnow in 1620s. [SCA.101]

WALWOOD, DAVID, in Kunow in 1651. [SCA.92]

WALWOOD, GEORGE, in Kunow in 1651. [SCA.92]

WALWOOD, THOMAS, a burgher of Opatow in 1659. [SCA.92/98]

WARDEN, DAVID, bound on a voyage to the Baltic in 1655, a case before the High Court of the Admiralty of Scotland on 18 December 1655. [NRS.AC2.1]

WARDROPER, GEORGE, master of the Robert and Mark of Arbroath, trading between Riga and Montrose in 1749; master of the Margaret of Dundee, trading between Danzig [Gdansk] and Dundee in 1743, with Riga in 1739, [NRS.E504.11.1; CE70.1.2]

WARDROPER, ROBERT, master of the Margaret of Dundee, trading between Riga and Dundee in 1747. [NRS.E504.11.2]

WATERSTONE, HANS or JOHN, a burgher and merchant of Linkoping, Sweden, around 1579, a merchant in Stockholm in 1582, trading illegally in Vadstena in 1579 and in 1587, an army officer in Livonia in the 1590s, he forfeited his estate in Vadstena in 1608. [SIS.23]

WATSON, ALBERT, married Katherine Guthrie, ['Gittre'], in the Burgkirche, Konigsberg, on 29 March 1644.

WATSON, JAMES, a merchant in Cullen, trading with Danzig [Gdansk] 1762-1766. [NRS.CS96.2919]

WATSON, JOHN, married Barbara Lenox, in the Burgkirche, Konigsberg, [Kaliningrad], on 20 January 1643.

WATSON, REGINA, in Vilnius, Lithuania, in 1641. [SCL.368]

WATSON, ROBERT, master of the Augusta of Montrose, trading between Memel [Klaipeda] and Montrose in 1765. [NRS.CE53.1.6]

WATSON, Captain, versus Cornelius Jansen, master of the Green Lion of Danzig, [Gdansk] in a petition before the High Court of the Admiralty of Scotland in 1710. [NRS.AC7.1]

WATT, ALEXANDER, married Greta Jeckfel, a widow, in St Elisabeth's, Danzig, on 2 March 1625.

WATT, ARCHIBALD, a Scot, married Catherina, daughter of Stenzel Neumann, in Altstadt, Konigsberg, [Kaliningrad], on 12 May 1611.

WATT, JAMES, master of the Robert of Leith, trading between Danzig [Gdansk] and Prestonpans in 1686. [NRS.E72.21.10]

WATT, JOHN, of Denmiln, a merchant in Dundee, trading with St Petersburg, Riga, Konigsberg, [Kaliningrad], Libau, [Liepaja], Archangel and Memel, [Klaipeda], between 1824 and 1829. [NRS.CS96.1329/2979]

WATT, MARIANA, a servant in Kedainiai, Lithuania, between 1679 and 1694. [SCL.368]

WATT, SAMUEL, master of the Liberty and Property, was contracted to ship goods from Danzig [Gdansk] by William Joseph and James Kenworthy, to Belfast for Daniel Mussenden, on 26 June 1756. [PRONI.D354.584]

WATT, WILLIAM, a servant in Kedainiai, Lithuania, in 1676-1679. [SCL.368]

WATT family, shipmasters in Dysart, trading with Archangel 1847, 1852, Riga 1847, 1849, 1851, Memel, [now Klaipeda],1848, 1849, Pillau, [now Baltiysk], 1849, Konigsberg, [now Kaliningrad] 1850, Narva, 1852, also Archangel, Stettin, [Szczecin]. [NRS.GD1.696.2]

WAUS, PATRICK, in Riga, letters, 1658-1659. [NRS.NRAS.2171.494]

WEBSTER, JAMES, master of the Nelly of Montrose, from Memel [Klaipeda] to Montrose in 1773. [NRS.CE53.1.8]

WEBSTER, THOMAS, master of the Nelly of Dundee, trading between Riga and Dundee in 1771. [NRS.E504.11.7]

WEBSTER ROBERT, master of the Two Brothers of Dundee, trading between Konigsberg [Kaliningrad] and Dundee in 1763, [NRS.E504.11.4]; master of the Barbara of Dundee, trading between Memel [Klaipeda] and Dundee in 1767, with Riga in 1768, 1769. [NRS.E504.11.7]

WEBSTER, THOMAS, master of the Jean of Montrose, trading between Riga and Montrose in 1758, and master of the Nelly, trading between Riga and Montrose in 1771. [NRS.CE53.1.5/8]

WEBSTER, Captain, master of the brig Aylesford of Dundee which was driven ashore on Faro, Gotland, when bound from St Petersburg to Arbroath in 1843. [MD.158]

'WEHLARDT, WILHELM', [?], a Scot, married Gertrud, daughter of Steffen Gross of Restenburg, on 3 May 1612.

WEIR, ROBERT, in Litomerice, a letter to the Marquis of Hamilton concerning the army in Silesia, dated 28 August 1634. [NRS.GD406.1.9319]

WHYTE, ALEXANDER, master of the Jean of Dundee, trading between Riga and Dundee in 1766, 1767; master of the Success of Dundee trading between Narva and Dundee in 1772, between Riga and Dundee in 1773, 1774, and between St Petersburg and Dundee in 1783. [NRS.E504.11.5/9/11]

WHITTET, JOHN, junior, a corn merchant in Dundee, trading with Libau, 1820-1821, a sederunt book. [NRS.CS96.3528]

WHITWORTH, Sir CHARLES, in St Petersburg, reports 1796, 1800, letters, 1800. [NRS.NRAS.3955/60/1/445-453; 11/8; 60/17/18]

WILKIE, JAMES, master of the James of Dumfries trading between Danzig, [Gdansk], and Dumfries in 1709. [CTB.24.118]

WILKIESON, ALEXANDER, son of John and Elisabeth Wilkieson in Edinburgh, was admitted as a citizen of Sandomierz in 1692. [SCA.96]

WILLIAMS, WILLIAM, [Wilhelm Wilhelms], a Scot, married Regina, widow of Lorenz Hasenfuss, in Altstadt, Konigsberg, [Kaliningrad], in 1605.

WILLIAMSON, DAVID, master of the Anna of Elie bound for Danzig on 24 February 1683. [NRS.E72.9.15]

WILLIAMSON, WILLIAM, a skipper in Kirkcaldy, master of the Gift of God entered a contract with some Edinburgh merchants, to take a cargo of coal to Konigsberg [Kaliningrad] or Danzig [Gdansk] and return with lint or coarse linen fibre, voyage abandoned, case before the High Court of the Admiralty of Scotland in 1631. [NRS.AC7.2.410]

WILLIAMSON, ..., master of the Thetis of Aberdeen was shipwrecked on a voyage to Danzig [Gdansk] on 15 October 1793. [AJ.2392]

WILLOX, ..., master of the Thetis of Aberdeen trading between Riga and Leith in 1783. [AJ.1853]

WILSON, CHARLES, master of the Elizabeth of Musselburgh, trading between Prestonpans and Danzig [Gdansk] in 1689. [NRS.E72.21.16]

WILSON, GEORGE, master of the Diligence of Peterhead, trading between Danzig [Gdansk] and Aberdeen in 1742. [NRS.E504.1.1]

WILSON, JOHN, in Vilnius, Lithuania, 1707-1708. [SCL.368]

WILSON, JOHN, a Scottish tailor, married Regina Aurin on 29 January 1657 in the Burgkirche, Konigsberg, [Kaliningrad].

WILSON or WILKIE, JOHN, master of the Isabel and Margaret of Leith, trading between Anstruther and Danzig [now Gdansk] in 1754. [NRS.E504.3.3]

WILSON, PETER, a Scot married Elisabeth Sinclair, widow of Robert Oliphant in Denmark, in St Elizabeth's, Danzig, [Gdansk], on 26 February 1634.

WINSTER, E., of the Scottish Brotherhood in Konigsberg in 1701. [SIG]

WISHART, ABRAHAM, husband of Madeline Fiddes, was admitted as a citizen of Lubowla in 1651, members of the Reformed Church in Cracow in the 1650s. [SAP.74]

WOOD, ALBERT, a merchant and citizen in Checiny between, 1633 and 1639. [SCA.89]

WOOD, [Wodt], BARTHOLEMEW, a merchant in Tarnow in the 1620s. [SCA.101]

WOOD, DAVID, master of the Patience of Montrose, trading between Montrose and Danzig [Gdansk] also Konigsberg [Kaliningrad] in 1684, 1685. [NRS.E72.16.15/16][RAK/STR]

WOOD, JAMES, master of the Jane of Pittenweem, trading between Perth and Danzig [now Gdansk] in 1745, 1749, with Riga in 1760, 1762, and the James of Pittenweem, trading between Anstruther and Danzig [now Gdansk] in 1748. [NRS.E504.27.2; E504.3.2/3]

WOOD, JOHN, in Rakow in 1691. [SCA.95]

WOOD, PETER, a citizen of Cracow in 1525. [SAP.70]

WORDIE, JOHN, a merchant in Edinburgh, and Antony Harrison, master of the Perth of Shields entered a charter party on 21 April 1778 for a voyage from Memel [Klaipedia] to Leith. [NRS.RH9.17.32.19]

WRIGHT, JOHN, [Hans Wrecht], a Scot, married Anna, daughter of Wilhelm Lichthun, in St Elizabeth's, Danzig, [Gdansk] on 23 September 1642.

WRIGHT, THOMAS, a merchant in Danzig, [now Gdansk], a sasine, 20 January 1774. [NRS.RS27.210.1]

WYLLIE, JAMES, born 2 January 1795, son of William Wyllie and his wife Annie Stupart, died in Russia on 21 October 1850. [Howff gravestone, Dundee]

YEAMAN, PATRICK, master of the Katherine of Dundee, trading between Dundee and Konigsberg [Kaliningrad] in 1684. [NRS.E72.7.13]

YELTON, JOHN, a merchant in Kincardine on Forth, trading with Memel and St Petersburg, 1798-1809. [NRS.CS96.58]

YOUNG, ADAM, a Scot, married Anna Bruns, in the Burgkirche, Konigsberg, [Kaliningrad], on 15 May 1639.

YOUNG, JAMES, [Jacon Junge], a Scottish tailor, married Cathrina Moltsfeld, on 25 April 1661 in the Burgkirche, Konigsberg, [Kaliningrad].

YOUNG, JAMES, master of the brig Industry of Dundee, from Riga to Dundee in 1796. [NRS.CE70.1.8/51]

YOUNG, JAMES, eight letters from the Crimean War, dated 1855-1856. [NRS.GD1.96.3]

YOUNG, JOHN, master of the Robert and John of Anstruther, trading between Anstruther and Danzig [now Gdansk] in 1749. [NRS.E504.3.3]

YOUNG, JOHN, master of the Kitty Graeme and Mary of Leith, trading between Danzig [Gdansk] and Aberdeen in 1743. [NRS.E504.1.1]

YOUNG, JOHN, master of the Betsy of Dundee trading between Riga and Dundee in 1775, 1776. [NRS.E504.11.8/9]

YOUNG, THOMAS, master of the Catherine of Dundee, trading between Narva and Dundee in 1761, with Memel [Klaipeda] in 1766, with Riga in 1767. [NRS.E504.11.4/6/7]

YOUNGER, GEORGE, master of the Lovely Peggie of Dundee, trading between Perth and Riga in 1764. [NRS.E504.27.4]

Some other shipping links-

Britannia of Dundee, was 'lost in the Baltic' in 1802. [NRS.CE70.1.10]

Edinburgh, a galley, from St Petersburg to Dundee in 1734. [MHS.183]

Euphemia of Dundee, was 'lost on the coast of Finland' in 1802. [DCA.CE70.1.10]

Expedient, a galley, from the Clyde to Archangel. [Scots Courant. 10 March 1711]

Fame of Dundee, was 'lost in the Baltic on her voyage from Dundee to St Petersburg' in 1800. [DCA.CE70.1.7]

Hope of Greenock, from the Clyde to Archangel. [Scots Courant. 9 June 1712]

James, from the Clyde to Archangel. [Scots Courant. 9 June 1712]

Jane, from the Clyde to Archangel in 1711, shipwrecked. [Scots Courant, 24 April 1711]

Vigilant of Port Glasgow, from the Clyde to Archangel. [Scots Courant.10 March 1711]

William of Leith was at Danzig [Gdansk] in September 1625. [PL.158]

A SAMPLE DOCUMENT

On 19 March 1631, James Nairn and Thomas Begg, merchants in Edinburgh, entered into a charter party with William Williamson, master of the Gift of God to take a cargo of coal from Leith to Konigsberg, Danzig, or other Baltic port, there to purchase lint, hards [ie coarse linen flax], pack goods, et cetera, and return to Leith. [NRS.AC7.4]